A Theology of the Subli

GW00499804

"... lucidly written, well structured and offers a sustained and engaging argument."

Paul Fletcher, *University of Lancaster*

"... addresses important issues in contemporary philosophy of religion and theology ... The ideas and arguments, particularly in which the exposition of Kant's notions of imagination and the sublime are related to current theological issues, are both topical and original."

James DiCenso, *University of Toronto*

A Theology of the Sublime is a response to the influential and controversial series, Radical Orthodoxy. Clayton Crockett develops a constructive radical theology from the philosophy of Immanuel Kant—a philosophy attacked by Radical Orthodoxy. Reading *The Critique of Judgment* back into *The Critique of Pure Reason*, and drawing upon the insights of such continental philosophers as Heidegger, Derrida, Lyotard and Deleuze, this book shows how existential notions of self, time, and imagination are interrelated in Kantian thinking, and demonstrates their importance for theology. An original theology of the sublime emerges as a connection is made between the Kantian sublime of the Third Critique and the transcendental imagination of the First Critique.

A Theology of the Sublime is a challenging and compelling argument for Kant's relevance to postmodern philosophy and contemporary theology. It raises critical questions about the nature and meaning of theological thinking and is the first major response to the Radical Orthodoxy movement.

Clayton Crockett is Visiting Assistant Professor of Modern Religious Thought at the College of William and Mary, Williamsburg, VA. He is the editor of *Secular Theology: American Radical Theological Thought*, also published by Routledge, and is managing editor of the online *Journal for Cultural and Religious Theory*.

A Theology of the Sublime

Clayton Crockett

London and New York

First published 2001
by Routledge
11 New Fetter Lane, London EC4P 4EE

Simultaneously published in the USA and Canada
by Routledge
29 West 35th Street, New York, NY 10001

Routledge is an imprint of the Taylor & Francis Group

© 2001 Clayton Crockett

Typeset in Sabon by
The Running Head Limited, Cambridge
Printed and bound in Great Britain by
Biddles Ltd, Guildford and King's Lynn

British Library Cataloguing in Publication Data
A catalogue record for this book is available from the British Library

Library of Congress Cataloging in Publication Data
A catalogue record for this book is available from the Library of Congress

ISBN 0–415–24093–X (hbk)
ISBN 0–415–24094–8 (pbk)

For Vicki, who means everything

Contents

Foreword by Charles E. Winquist   ix
Acknowledgments   xiii

Introduction   1

1 Kantian critical philosophy as theology   9

2 On modern sublimity: the challenge of Radical
   Orthodoxy   23

3 Ontology and linguistics: Heidegger and Lyotard   37

4 Temporality, subjectivity and imagination: Kant *avec*
   Deleuze   51

5 The Analytic of the Sublime   67

6 The transcendental imagination   85

7 Towards a theology of the sublime   99

Notes   113
Bibliography   129
Index   137

Foreword

A Theology of the Sublime is a book about Immanuel Kant and Paul Tillich. It is explicitly a reading and interpretation of Kant's *Critique of Pure Reason* and *Critique of Judgment* with special attention to the notions of the imagination and the sublime. It is implicitly a reading of Kant beside the specter of Tillich's theology of ultimate concern. Tillich speaks in the interstices of a rethinking of Kant. Tillich's demands on theology are read beside Kant's philosophy in a way that Crockett is able to understand Kant's critical philosophy as theology. Crockett critically reads the First Critique forward into the Third Critique and the Third Critique backward into the First Critique. This is complicated by a further forward reading of Kantianism into postmodern thinking and postmodern sensibilities into Kantianism. He reads Kant next to Heidegger, Derrida, Deleuze, Lyotard, and Vattimo. Through the openings of these many readings it makes sense to think the meaning of an ultimate concern and the sometimes hidden Tillich reappears.

Crockett does not confuse the transcendental with the transcendent and thus reads Kant's idealism as a radical empiricism deeply responsive to David Hume. What might appear as metaphysical in Kant is more importantly understood as metaphorical by Crockett. Understanding the Kantian transcendental imagination as closely akin to Derridian *différance* is a Kantian theme that has not been fully experienced or appreciated by many readers of Kant or Derrida. This opens the possibility for valuing ultimate concern as a quasi-transcendental condition for subjectivity. For Crockett this recognition frees theological discourse to investigate other terms, other powers, and other experiences for their sense and significance. For him this is a move against both dogmatism and Radical Orthodoxy.

What he understands as a metaphorical deepening of thought is intercalated with Charles Long's minimal definition of religion as an orientation to reality in an ultimate sense. The words that are difficult in this definition are *ultimate* and *sense*. The orientation that Crockett accesses and assesses is the theological disorientation that occurs through a serious understanding of the Kantian understanding of the sublime. The Kantian notion of the sublime is an extreme example of disorientation because it is not able to be sublated under the concepts of the understanding. There are experiences that are problems without solutions. Serious thinking can be a driftwork.

Crockett recognizes that there are resistances to what he recognizes in the formulation of the Kantian problematic and in the recognition that sometimes we have to think under conditions not of our own choosing. In what might first appear as an aside, he criticizes Radical Orthodoxy through its representation in the works of John Milbank and Phillip Blond. Crockett resists the idea that there can be a move to a post-secular philosophy or theology because this move misunderstands the importance of the Kantian sublime by confusing it with an object rather than identifying the experience of the sublime with the subject's conflict of faculties in perceiving such an object. He respects the integrity and rigor in the formulations of Radical Orthodoxy as it articulates a theological agenda but at the same time argues that we cannot dismiss the understanding of the Kantian relocation of God or the sublime into the internal realm of transcendental conditions for subjectivity. We cannot confuse the sublime with a transcendent object. These transcendental or quasi-transcendental conditions show themselves in a Deleuzian understanding of Kant as a swerve which is itself a condition for fruitful thinking but such a swerve is thought in Radical Orthodoxy as the uncertainty that is a nihilism.

Crockett's fine-grained analyses of Kantian texts read alongside of Heideggerian, Lyotardian, Deleuzian, and Derridian texts show that the production of knowledge is primordial and complex and cannot be dismissed by privileging any particular revelation or theological thematic. There are *differends* and phrases are in dispute. There is a splitting of the Kantian subject into a passive self that appears as an object of representation and an active self that performs the representing. The problem is that these selves are not identical. At best there can be a discordant accord.

There is no single apprehension or productive comprehension that unifies the faculties of mind. Reason can think the concept of the mathematical sublime but it cannot subsume the dynamic sublime under its concepts. The Enlightenment confidence in reason is undermined by its own achievement. As Crockett argues, "the sublime reveals the negative power of the imagination—not the inability of the imagination to give form, but the disturbing ability of imagination to engender form beyond the ability of understanding to represent and reason to contain." Kant cannot preserve the sovereignty of understanding. The very procedure or process of representation cannot itself be represented. This is a lesson of the dynamic sublime and is an enigma for theology.

As Crockett demonstrates, the Kantian enigma for theology is formal or in more traditional terms epistemological. There is no privileged content that makes it go away. Even revelation would have to be received under the human conditions of thinking. Even the concept *God* is subject to temporalization and subjectivization in being thought.

Religion is in some sense what we cannot think. Crockett reads this as an expression of Tillich's understanding of depth and writes that "One can identify a sphere or phenomenon as religion only when its self-representation breaks down." The depth of religion is an abyss which is a surface complexity in any sphere of culture that defies comprehension.

Crockett concludes his book by reading Kantianism into Freudian psycho-analytic theory. The Kantian sublime refigures the negative imagination as a desire that fissures subjectivity.

Crockett's new theology is restless and open. Deconstructive thinking is the possibility for reconstructive thinking. This new theology denies denial. There is no thinking that is not thinking. The theology of the sublime is an acknowledgment of an epistemological exigency that is a theological exigency in thinking. The problematic that he articulates is a hopefulness that forecloses closure.

Charles E. Winquist
Syracuse University
Syracuse, New York, USA

Acknowledgments

The Department of Religion at Syracuse University supported and encouraged me throughout my graduate education, and I particularly want to acknowledge James B. Wiggins, Richard Pilgrim, David L. Miller, and Carol Williams. A Syracuse University Dissertation Fellowship in 1997–8 afforded me the opportunity to complete my dissertation and begin significant revisions.

I want to thank James J. DiCenso for his criticism and comments on an earlier draft, as well as an additional anonymous reader for Routledge for suggestions which helped to shape the final version. The editorial staff at Routledge have been extremely helpful and friendly, including Roger Thorp, Hywel Evans, Adrian Driscoll, and Anna Gerber.

I would also like to thank James C. Livingston and Robert P. Scharlemann for their teaching and general influence on my thinking. Gregg Lambert has provided invaluable suggestions and guidance concerning this book, as well as theoretical and practical advice in general, and I am pleased to acknowledge him as a spiritual older brother. I am indebted to many friends and colleagues for conversations and advice concerning the ideas in this book, and I especially want to thank Martin Kavka, Oz Lorentzen, Noëlle Vahanian and Paul Miranda. My family has been incredibly supportive of my work, including Becky Crockett, Bill Crockett, Clint Crockett, Tollie Spivey and Paulette Bryan. My advisor, mentor, fellow theologian, and above all friend, Charles E. Winquist, deserves credit for much of the originality of this book, and his inspiration and example provide a foundation upon which to think and write. Finally, as the dedication attests, I could not have accomplished this without the love of my wife Vicki Bryan Crockett, whose belief in me is amazing and unsurpassed.

Introduction

> Religion is conscientiousness. The holiness of the acceptance and the truth-fulness of what man must confess to himself. Confess to yourself. To have religion, the concept of God is not required (still less the postulate: "There is a God").
>
> Immanuel Kant, *Opus Postumum*

Because we think, human beings raise theological questions, which is not to say that we necessarily possess answers to these questions. To ask about the significance of anything in an ultimate or fundamental sense is to ask a theological question. This is what Paul Tillich means by defining theology as "ultimate concern." To ask a question and not to possess an immediate answer opens the space for theological thinking to occur. For Christians, if "it is accomplished" (John 19: 30), if revelation is truly complete, then all theological reflection is not merely irrelevant but impossible. Theological inquiry may begin with a claim of revelation, or the actuality of an event, but it cannot be securely harnessed to it, because such inquiry ultimately exceeds such bounds and interrogates the conditions of possibility of an actual event. Theology may proceed to inquire whether such conditions actually constitute the *impossibility* of that event, or even whether the event actually happened. Theology always threatens to exceed the bounds of revelation, which is why institutions (both ecclesiastical and academic) are constrained to devise methods to keep it in check.

Representatives of dogmatic institutions promote confessional theologies which serve the interests of already-established interpretations, and such theologies comfort lay members of such institutions who would sooner allay doubts and discrepancies than open them up. In this sense (confessional or apologetic), theology is inherently conservative. On the other hand, a radical theological thinking itself raises unsettling issues which demand an engagement with idealities of discourses and materialities of culture (and vice versa) in order to cultivate a theological vision, or what

Deleuze and Guattari call an "image of thought" which would be relent-lessly honest in relation to the theological questioning. What would a theological thinking look like for which everything is at stake, precisely because nothing is settled?

Such a radical theology must assemble the terms and distinctions it wields as it goes along. It does not foreclose entanglements with alternative discourses, especially philosophical discourses. This book represents a theo-logical experiment, which seeks to assemble or construct a theology of the sublime out of what is ultimately a theological encounter with Kant's Critiques of Reason and Judgment. Kant does not represent an arbitrary choice. In many ways, he is the paradigmatic thinker of modernity, and his theoretical achievements and distinctions have affected any intellectual who writes after him. A theological encounter with Kant presents a test-case of modernity, and the stakes of any possible modern or even postmodern theological thinking.

Most scholars would not dispute the claim that Immanuel Kant is con-sidered the greatest modern philosopher, and his *Critique of Pure Reason* the most important philosophical work of modernity. Kant also represents the culmination of the Western European Enlightenment.[1] In his master-work, Kant investigates and sets forth the transcendental conditions which determine the possibility of knowledge of an object. His "Copernican revolution" establishes that in our knowing, objects conform to the laws of human understanding rather than vice versa.[2]

Unfortunately, however, many contemporary commentators in their quest to determine the exact logical status of Kant's arguments have missed, over-looked, or set aside the radicality of Kant's questions and formulations.[3] In a similar manner, the major representatives of the Anglo-American philo-sophical tradition, philosophers such as P.F. Strawson, Jonathan Bennett, Paul Guyer, and Henry Allison, have been more passionate about evaluat-ing the accuracy or adequacy of Kant's conclusions based upon the current state of science and philosophy of language in the twentieth century than in grappling with the challenges for thinking which Kant opens up.[4]

In order to engage more fully the Kant whom Moses Mendelssohn labeled "all-destroying,"[5] I have turned to the works of contemporary continental philosophers, such as Martin Heidegger, Jean-François Lyotard, Gilles Deleuze, and Jacques Derrida. For these thinkers, Kant's work ex-erts a power and a pressure on their own thinking. None of them could be said to endorse Kant's ideas and solutions in an unqualified manner, but their engagement with Kantian ideas opens up and provides a crucial impetus for the formation of their philosophy. In this spirit, and coincident with the significance of language for philosophy in the twentieth century, one could revisit Hans Vaihinger's statement that "to the slogan 'Kant as metaphysician' one can just as well counterpose the slogan 'Kant as metaphorician.'"[6] For this reading, the choice must be refused whether to read Kant as metaphysician *or* metaphorician; rather, the two must be seen to be fused in the generation of philosophical ideas.

My intention here is to read Kantian critical philosophy as theology. That is, I want to read Kant under the pressure of theological notions such as "ultimate concern." Any Kantian theology would have to be in many respects a formal theology, or a theology which is theological in form rather than simply in content. Kant examines the formal conditions of knowledge in abstraction from any empirical content. A content-driven theology would examine religious texts for ideas about God, salvation, ultimate reality, etc., but a formal or form-driven theology could read other texts, including philosophical texts, and pressure their arguments with issues of "ultimate concern," "importance," "meaning," and others.

The first chapter is an articulation and justification of reading Kantian critical philosophy as theology. Here a broad trajectory of theological thinking is sketched out in which the object of theology becomes more and more formal. Chapter Two represents an engagement with, and critique of, Cambridge Radical Orthodoxy, particularly theologians like John Milbank who contend that Kant is the prime representative of a secular atheistic modernity as well as the *bête noire* of constructive postmodern theology. For Milbank, modern sublimity refers to a viewpoint which loses sight of God's transcendence in a rational and positive way, and can only perceive God as terrifying and irrational. Unfortunately, Milbank and others fail to understand the Kantian sublime profoundly enough, because they take it as referring more to an external object rather than a process internal to thinking.

The critique of Radical Orthodoxy sets up an interpretation against which I develop my own reading of the Kantian sublime in the context of contemporary continental thinkers. In Chapter Three, the interpretations of Heidegger and Lyotard are laid out and interrogated in order to provide a foundation for carefully rereading the *Critique of Pure Reason* and the *Critique of Judgment*. Heidegger demonstrates the importance of temporality and the productive power of imagination for the First Critique, especially as they construct human subjectivity, or *Dasein*. Lyotard focuses on the *Critique of Judgment*, which Heidegger neglects, and constructs a model of reflective judgment which he then claims is a better model for knowing than objective judgment by means of the categories, or the pure concepts of the understanding, developed in the First Critique.

Heidegger provides a new way of reading and understanding the First Critique. Lyotard asserts the significance of the Third Critique, and imports, as it were, the Kantian critical project of the *Critique of Pure Reason* into the *Critique of Judgment*. Building on Heidegger and Lyotard, and using the insights of Deleuze and Derrida, I read the *Critique of Judgment* back into the *Critique of Pure Reason*, and I suggest that this attempt poses serious consequences for Kantian philosophy as a whole. This interpretation of Kant makes up the core of the book, Chapters Four through Six. The reading is a critical reading, which is in some ways a reading of Kant's latent implications against Kant's manifest conclusions. Perhaps more importantly, however, my interpretation represents the isolation or elaboration of a certain tension which drives the Kantian project even as it compromises some of its results. This tension can most closely be identified with the term imagination, or *Einbildungskraft*, as a form-giving power, but more in its negative than in its positive role.[7]

My contention is that the disappearance of the understanding in the sublime judgment, in the *Critique of Judgment*, points to the breakdown of the understanding not only in the Third Critique but also, and more importantly, in the *Critique of Pure Reason*. The desperate struggle between reason and imagination in the judgment of the sublime, when considered in terms of the determinate judgment of objective knowledge of the understanding of the First Critique, writes large the problems surrounding the transcendental imagination as it appears in the Transcendental Deduction of the categories and then most importantly in the Transcendental Schematism. The inability to reproduce or image a schema, because of the temporality of the act of understanding, severely compromises or undoes the objectivity of the understanding Kant desperately wants to establish in the realm of appearances. The problem of the Schematism, which is also the transcendental imagination, also inscribes into thinking a profound epistemological and theological problem. This is a wound of thinking which drives both Derrida's notion of *différance* and Deleuze's thinking of difference or differentiation in their respective philosophies. This Kantian wound is one which has not been fully experienced or grappled with, although in many ways it has determined the possibilities for philosophical and theological thinking ever since.

The significance of the transcendental imagination in the Schematism has important implications for theology. Chapter Seven reflects upon the consequences of such a rereading of Kant for contemporary theological thinking. I articulate a theology of the sublime as form in relation to formlessness, which is not simply a formal theology. In addition, I connect Kant's conflict of the faculties, as understood and expressed by Deleuze, with Tillich's understanding of religion as the depth aspect of human spiritual life, whether in its cognitive, moral, or aesthetic functions. The theological significance of a proliferation and/or breakdown of form, suggested by the importance of imagination as form-building, is considered, as well as implications for understanding human subjectivity. This rethinking of Kantian notions of imagination, temporality, and subjectivity, specifically understood in terms of the Schematism and the sublime, is intended as a creative spur towards new possibilities for theological thinking, in relation to such discourses as anthropology and psychoanalysis. Such thinking would take up the questions of subjectivity, representation, creative imagination, and thinking in all of their power and complexity and imagine them anew.

This book, then, is not simply a reading of Kant; it is also a study of theological method. Unfortunately, this work would not be recognized as anything other than philosophy by much of what passes for theology in current intellectual circles. Nevertheless, I place myself within a particular theological tradition, which is a radical Tillicheanism that includes American Death of God theology.

Here, the "Death of God" does not pass judgment upon the reality of God in any ultimate way; it functions to free theological discourse to investigate other terms, other powers, and other expressions for their sense and significance. In this study of Kant, the self or subjectivity is the key locus of concern, or the central theological site of investigation. For Tillich, our understanding of the self furnishes information of the receptacle of revelation, which is to say that it determines the form that faith takes. A theological inquiry which brackets its relation to both God and world in order to trace its modern constitution in Kantian thought, provides a radical transformation of our understanding of subjectivity. This transformed subjectivity then pressures any understanding of faith and religion.

Much contemporary theology which identifies itself as such is reactionary and dogmatic, which prevents any serious grappling with the real issues and problems of thought which confront modern and postmodern societies. Even Barthianism, which defines the possibilities for current theological debate to a great extent, eclipses the radicality Barth fashioned his theology with, which is in many respects a great modern theology. Most orthodox theologies in any case suffer from one crucial shortcoming taken from Barth, which is the restriction of any authentic theologizing to the churches. Not only does this exclude the possibility of any academic theology, and subordinate academic intellectual activity to the demands of an ecclesiastical community, but it disallows any decisive confrontation with the powerful ideological, technological, and economic forces which shape the possibilities for faith and thinking.

On the other hand, much progressive or liberation theology has praiseworthy goals, but in its anti-intellectualism it subordinates theoretical to practical concerns, and dilutes its significance. Such liberation theology often overlooks the power and insights of those figures whose theories have provided its primary impetus. The point is not to oppose practice to theory, or alternatively to reverse the relationship so that "theory" is sovereign in relation to "praxis," but to think critically beyond such simple-minded oppositions. Theology nearly everywhere mistakes piety for faith, realizing without fully understanding the extent to which thinking is a threat to simple-minded faith, and that genuine faith is a torturous struggle. Many people feel the need to have consolation and reassurance as they struggle with their faith, their lives, and their dreams in a postmodern, technocratic society, but to confine theology to this reassuring moment of faith that justifies piety in intellectualist terms cheapens faith itself and again forecloses any radical theological thinking, which is a process rather than a result.

In the United States, religion and spirituality are extremely popular and of concern to many, but this desire for comfort, the need to feel something more than one's own mundane existence, rarely takes the form of serious thinking and questioning at the level of textual discourse (which is not to say that it does not take place existentially). A symptom of this situation is the marginalization of philosophy and theory in discourse about religion, which is mirrored in academia by a backlash against theory in departments of religion and elsewhere. As a result, theology becomes defensive and is left anemic, such that only in historical studies can one admit that canonical figures such as Aristotle, Augustine, Thomas Aquinas, Martin Luther, etc., were extraordinary thinkers who radically altered theology because of their immersion in contemporary intellectual issues, which again does not mean that they thereby ignored social, political, practical, and other concerns.

In a post-Kantian intellectual world, theologians cannot simply assume immediate access to the objects of faith without accounting for the irreducibly subjective nature of the constitution of such objects. As an instigation to serious theological reflection, I engage Kant as a powerful and paradigmatic thinker, and this engagement gives rise to a conception of the sublime, which is used to interrogate contemporary discourses and make inquiries concerning the generation of theological meaning. Conservative theologies want to preserve the forms of traditional theological debate, and above all the form of theology, but I want to risk the very form of theology in order to ask if we can meaningfully think theologically today.

Therefore, my use of philosophy and philosophers is not restricted to a classical disciplinary conception, and in fact my models here are Deleuze and Derrida, two thinkers who have radically exposed and questioned philosophy in what is sometimes seen as a deformation, in the monstrous sense of the word. One should have the courage and the honesty not merely to apply the results of this "French postmodernism" to theology and theological figures in what is often called the deconstruction of metaphysics, which essentially leaves one's own theology (identified with faith) untouched, but rather to undertake a questioning no less intense, probing and serious in and of one's own theology. There is a demand to be self-critical in the way that Tillich suggests in his formulation of what he calls the "Protestant principle," which protests "against the identification of our ultimate concern with any creation of the church, including the biblical writings."[8] The risks are tremendous, and one exposes oneself to charges of nihilism if one attempts to take seriously, to grapple with and diagnose the "nihilism" inherent in our contemporary situation and thinking, which may in fact harbor uncanny and revelatory new meanings. Nietzsche is usually called a nihilist, precisely because he uncovers what he calls "European nihilism" and challenges himself to tackle it head-on in order to find a way through it, not a detour around or a retreat back out of it. At the same time, Nietzsche is the thinker who attempted the most far-reaching spiritual affirmation in his formulation of *amor fati*:

> My formula for greatness in a human being is *amor fati*: that one wants nothing to be other than it is, not in the future, not in the past, not in all eternity. Not merely to endure what happens of necessity, still less to dissemble it—all idealism is untruthfulness in the face of necessity—but to *love* it.[9]

1 Kantian critical philosophy as theology

Introduction

What are the possibilities for theological thinking at the turning of the millennium? What resources does Kantian philosophy provide for a theology which attempts to be intellectually responsible in an academic and secular manner? This chapter develops these questions in the course of a coarse-grained analysis which paints in broad strokes some of the historical, philosophical, and theological developments of Western European modernity in order to provide a context for a constructive understanding of theology. This coarse-grained analysis also lays the ground for a more fine-grained analysis of Kant's thought later in the book.[1]

I

In his introduction to *Theology at the End of the Century*, Robert P. Scharlemann points out "several distinguishing features of the postmodern in its significance for theological thinking."[2] Here Scharlemann sets out the questioning of the transparency of the self, the Nietzschean declaration of the death of God, the Hegelian transformation of the speculative Good Friday into world history, and the loss of first principles, as characteristics of postmodernity. Here I am primarily concerned with the first of these features, the questioning of the transparency of the self. Scharlemann suggests that the "full transparency of the self to itself in thinking" is a Cartesian notion, but it also applies to "the Kantian notion of the apperception of the transcendental ego."[3]

In his book, *Erring: A Postmodern A/theology*, Mark C. Taylor also identifies four characteristics of postmodernity which are important for theological thinking: the Death of God, the Disappearance of the Self, the End of History, and the Closure of the Book. These four features are similar but not identical to those delineated by Scharlemann. Taylor addresses what he calls the disappearance of the self by emphasizing the irreducible complexity and plurality over the identity and unity of the self. Appealing to Hegel, Taylor claims that "there is no identity without repetition. Something can be itself only by doubling itself."[4] The inevitable temporality of selfhood precludes simple and total identity. I am not evaluating the claim that the self has "disappeared," only pointing out both the significance and the contested nature or status of self and subjectivity in contemporary theological thinking.

For me, the term "postmodern" primarily refers not to the validity of any of the above claims, nor to any others which supposedly characterize "postmodernism," but rather to a method for asking questions about the nature and stakes of modernity. For the Italian philosopher Gianni Vattimo, the "post-modern" is characterized by a calling into question of the value of the modern, or the new and up-to-date as such. This occurs paradigmatically in Nietzsche's philosophy, according to Vattimo. Such a calling into question of the modern is not a reactionary opposition that merely attempts to overcome modernity and replace it with another value-system. For Vattimo, Nietzsche is significant because he "brings into play a true dissolution of modernity through a radicalization of its own constitutive tendencies."[5]

Therefore, a genuine postmodernism cannot simply be opposed to modernity. However, if modernity itself can be questioned, that questioning implies a distance between the "modern" and the person raising the question of the value and significance of modernity. In this case, a postmodern theological thinking can relate itself to modernity in a complex way by engaging the paradigmatic thinker of the Western Enlightenment, Immanuel Kant.

The contested nature of the self testifies to its theological significance, and in some ways a modern understanding of the self has to do not only with Descartes but also with Kant's theoretical philosophy. On the one hand, one can rationally formulate the significance of subjectivity in terms of reflexivity, that is, that entity which asks questions about the meaning of its existence. This is Heidegger's concept of *Dasein*, which he develops in *Being and Time*. The being of *Dasein*, or the being of that entity which asks questions about the significance of its own being-in-the-world, is care, Heidegger concludes.[6] This care of, or concern with, self and subjectivity is central to the philosophical and theological thinking of modernity.

On the other hand, a concern with self and subjectivity can be deduced based on the importance and controversy the idea takes on in contemporary intellectual discussions. The concept of subjectivity can be seen as a central value for modernity as well as a contested term in contemporary debates. At one extreme, Michel Foucault is understood as announcing the death of the self when in *The Order of Things* he describes "man" as a footprint on a beach between two tides; that is, the human self or species is a concept recently invented and destined soon to perish.[7] On the other hand, Charles Taylor and Seyla Benhabib more carefully articulate a complex understanding of human ethical selfhood in its relation to community.[8] Finally, a recent discussion of subjectivity and German philosophy, with particular reference to Kant, occurs in *The Modern Subject: Conceptions of the Self in Classical German Philosophy*. This volume brings together continental German scholarship with contemporary analytic philosophy, in an attempt to fend off "the tendencies of current philosophy, which are very critical, and even antagonistic to, subjectivity."[9] The development of my analysis of post-Kantian continental philosophy suggests that it is a facile interpretation of philosophers such as Heidegger, Lyotard, Derrida, and Deleuze to state that they wish to get rid of or dismiss the subject or subjectivity, although they do complicate it for intellectuals working with more traditional paradigms. My claim is that the status of the modern subject is an important component of any contemporary theology, and that Kantian philosophy represents a central formulation of human subjectivity. By investigating and interrogating Kant's framework of the self, which also involves temporality and imagination, we can clarify the situation for making important theological inquiries.

II

The self's status as a central value also constitutes a key locus of concern, which I want to relate to Paul Tillich's notion of ultimate concern. Tillich defines religion as ultimate concern. In Volume One of his *Systematic Theology*, which is partly influenced by Heidegger's *Being and Time*, Tillich's "second formal criterion of theology" states: "Our ultimate concern is that which determines our being and non-being. Only those statements are theological which deal with their object in so far as it can become a matter of being or not-being for us."[10] Insofar as ultimate concern "determines our being and non-being," human beings are ultimately concerned with their own identity as a self. This is a theological statement, for Tillich. Theology consists in a second-order reflection upon religious experience. Religion or religious experience is immediately concerned existence, and is related implicitly to an ultimate concern. The task of theology is to explicitly theorize the content of that ultimate concern. As we will see, however, ultimate concern does not possess any simple content.

For Tillich, religion is defined as ultimate concern. In his *Systematic Theology*, "ultimate concern is unconditional, independent of any conditions of character, desire, or circumstance."[11] Furthermore, this ultimate concern is total and infinite. Tillich argues that the "word 'concern' points to the 'existential' character of religious experience."[12] Everyone is religious in some way, because everybody has some amount of concern or care. But only an "ultimate" concern can be identified with religion properly so-called, and for Tillich theology represents the second-order study of this religious experience, in terms of the evaluation of claims for ultimacy on the part of any of its concerns.

Tillich claims that religion is the depth dimension of human life. In his *Theology of Culture*, the metaphor of depth means "that which is ultimate, infinite, unconditional" in human spiritual life.[13] Theological reflection follows upon the experiential aspect of human existence in the world, which for Tillich is religious existence, because it is concerned existence. For Tillich, the "first formal criterion of theology" reads:

> The object of theology is what concerns us ultimately. Only propositions are theological which deal with their object in so far as it can become a matter of ultimate concern for us.[14]

Does our concerned existence have an object which can be called an ultimate concern?

God is the only proper object of ultimate concern. Tillich claims, however, that one can do no more than symbolize this ultimate reality, or God, which he identifies philosophically with being-itself. In his *Dynamics of Faith* he says that "everything which is a matter of unconditional concern is made into a god."[15] But this process of making a determinate object into an ultimate concern is idolatrous, and therefore demonic for Tillich, who strives to hold onto the metaphorical nature of the symbols used to speak about ultimate reality. The self cannot be called an ultimate concern either, unless one considers it unconditional, total, and infinite.

Recall, however, that Tillich's theological criterion is a *formal* criterion. He also claims later in *Systematic Theology* that "nothing can appear in the theological system which transcends the whole of experience."[16] An ultimate concern cannot be one concern among others in the midst of human experience, because no human experience, value or concern in itself can be total, infinite, and unconditional. Any empirical concern which is identified as an ultimate concern would be for Tillich idolatrous. The notion of ultimate concern pressures in a transcendental way the existence and claim for ultimacy of every empirical concern. As Charles E. Winquist writes, "this criterion [Tillich's first formal criterion for theology] functions as an interrogative demand and implicates theology in existential value decisions."[17]

Tillich appears to be writing a transcendental theology which deals with the possibility of religious experience. Kant, in a similar way, states at the beginning of the *Critique of Pure Reason* that "there can be no doubt that all our knowledge begins with experience," (B1) and he elaborates his critique by establishing the transcendental conditions by which any object can be known as an object of possible experience. Things as they are in themselves, however, cannot be known in any certain, dogmatic, or transcendent way; this could only be known by an intellectual intuition, and is impossible for finite human knowledge (Bxl). In fact, any claim to knowledge of things-in-themselves, by making the transcendental ideas of God, self, and world objects of possible experience rather than ideas which regulate our experience of objects in the world, represents a dialectical illusion which Kant attempts to expose and deny. Our empirical representations of self can neither be hypostasized into transcendent reality, nor taken as a locus of ultimate concern. In its transcendental function, however, as a concept or idea which pressures our understanding and our values, subjectivity can be examined or interrogated in terms of or in light of its ultimacy.

Tillich is the central representative of a theologian in this book because his theology is sufficiently formal or minimal enough to allow theology to open itself up to contemporary culture and its theoretical expressions. Tillich does not wall his theology off from culture and philosophy, and he is willing to risk the form of theology itself by meditating on the possibility for theology to be relevant and meaningful, that is, to orient itself towards a concerned existence. By focusing on the form of Tillich's theology, I am able to isolate a certain Kantianism which drives his thinking, and this reading of ultimate concern as a transcendental condition of theological thinking propels me towards what is ultimately a theological reading of Kant himself.

Tillich's systematic theology is in many important ways a formal theology, just as Kant's philosophy is a formal philosophy.[18] Both abstract the conditions for the possibility of an experience as the form that experience can take, from the possible content of an experience. In discussing morality, Tillich claims that "while morality as the pure form of existential self-affirmation is absolute, the concrete systems of moral imperatives, the 'moralisms,' are relative."[19] His justification of this assertion is Kantian, because Tillich writes that the separation of form, which is necessary, from content, which is arbitrary, is "the acknowledgment of man's [sic] finitude and his dependence on the contingencies of time and space."[20] Kant distinguishes the necessary formal conditions for knowing from the arbitrary contents of knowledge, and in the Transcendental Aesthetic the two pure, universal, and aesthetic forms which intuitions take are time and space. Every object which is an object of human perception or intuition must appear in the form of time and space. For Kant, space is the form of all appearances of outer sense, that is, external sensations, while time is the "form of inner sense, that is, of the intuition of ourselves and of our inner state" (A33/B50). This attention to the form of our knowledge and experience is characteristic of European modernity, in both philosophy and theology.

III

According to Jürgen Habermas, the history of philosophy can in a very general sense be divided into three periods and/or types: philosophies of being, philosophies of consciousness, and philosophies of language.[21] Although Habermas deals primarily with the transition from philosophies of consciousness to philosophies of language, Descartes is the paradigmatic figure representing the transition from a philosophy of being, which deals with the substance of reality, to a philosophy of consciousness which addresses the receptacle, or human form of intuiting that reality. A philosophy of language, identified with Nietzsche, attends to the material and formal linguisiticality of our conscious expressions and intuitions. In this way, philosophy becomes more and more formal, focusing on the formal conditions for knowledge rather than simply the object or contents of that knowledge. Kant represents an important stage in this development, because he abstracts the pure form of experience in both our knowing and our acting, and empties it of any necessary content. Kant does not get rid of the contents of experience; we cannot have an experience without any content whatsoever. What Kant relativizes is the particularity of any content of knowledge or experience while he universalizes the form of that knowing experience. This move becomes extremely clear regarding Kant's morality in the *Critique of Practical Reason*. The universal moral law is the maxim to act such that every action could become the subject of a universal moral law. This universality, however, cannot apply to any particular empirical law.

> Therefore, a rational being either cannot think of his subjective practical principles (maxims) as at the same time universal laws, or he must suppose that their mere *form*, through which they are fitted for being given as universal laws, is alone that which makes them a practical law [emphasis mine].[22]

Only the legislative form makes a moral law universal and valid. So one cannot prescribe contents, but only the universal form, of any pure moral law, which is also what Tillich claims.

During the course of its historical development, Western philosophy becomes formal, in that it attends more and more to the material conditions for human knowing and existence. Philosophy also becomes more formal in that knowledge of an object becomes more and more problematic, and the object dissolves, as it were, under the gaze of skeptical philosophical inquiry. Hume's investigations stress the psychological and subjective necessity of the observer to impose necessity upon an event. In any understanding of causality, he demonstrates that an appeal is made to forces whose existence and necessary connection cannot be proved, only trusted with greater and lesser amounts of probability.[23] Hume's problem regarding the objective nature of causality stimulates Kant's efforts to secure objective theoretical knowledge, lest one fall into skepticism. Kant's solution, however, is to divide knowledge of objects into objects as they appear to human perception, and objects as they are in themselves.

> As appearances, they [objects] cannot exist in themselves, but only in us. What objects may be in themselves, and apart from all this receptivity of our sensibility, remains completely unknown to us. We know nothing but our mode of perceiving them—a mode which is peculiar to us, and not necessarily shared by every being, though, certainly, by every human being.
>
> (A42/B59)

Kant ultimately adopts a Humean solution regarding the phenomenality of objects, claiming that our own understanding supplies the necessary laws by which objects can be known. Kant states this conclusion clearly in his *Prolegomena to any Future Metaphysics*. "The highest legislation of nature must lie in ourselves," Kant writes, "that is, in our understanding . . . we must not seek the universal laws of nature in nature by means of experience, but conversely must seek nature, as to its universal conformity to law, in the conditions of the possibility of experience which lie in our sensibility and in our understanding."[24] The fact that objects have a separate existence, apart from our knowledge of them, introduces a new form of skepticism which Kant tries to contain by calling transcendental idealism.

By calling attention to the importance of form in the history of philosophy, and particularly for Kant, I want to make an analogy to the development of Protestant theology since the Reformation. Attention to this development demonstrates the importance of theological form for a theologian like Tillich, and raises the possibility of a formal theology of ultimate concern abstracted from any necessary content.

The beginnings of historical and philological criticism in the Renaissance with figures like Lorenzo Valla and Erasmus provided the tools for Protestant reform.[25] Martin Luther, trained in the *via moderna*, challenged the authority of the Roman Catholic Church in a dramatic and successful way, which brought about the dissolution of a dominant form of Christendom in Europe. Luther's famous slogan, "salvation by grace through faith alone," without the possibility of being justified by works, was accompanied by an appeal to Scripture as the main locus of authority, once the Church's hegemony had been shattered.[26]

The unleashing of critical forces, however, quickly threatened the security of any intellectual refuge in the literality of the Bible. In the German

Enlightenment, rationalist biblical criticism had a great impact, especially the writings of J.S. Semler and the fragments of H.S. Reimarus, discovered and published by G.E. Lessing.[27] These writings challenged not only the historical veracity of the Christian Old Testament, but also the unity of the four gospel narratives, and paved the way for much more sophisticated and devastating critiques of the New Testament.[28] The object of traditional theology, the Word of God, dissolves under the gaze of modern biblical criticism, despite current attempts by post-liberals such as George Lindbeck and Stanley Hauerwas to salvage the Gospel narratives as incommensurable and self-insulating by ignoring any external critical questions and problems.

Theology has never possessed a simple object. Even the Bible functioned metonymically for scholars and theologians like John Calvin, who imported Renaissance concerns and influential writers of antiquity like Plato and Cicero into the scriptures.[29] But the crisis of theology not having a viable object, except in a reactionary and anti-modern way, may never have been so acute as it is at present. Theology cannot save itself by reconstituting its object in a reactionary and traditional manner, in defiance of all scholarly norms, if it desires to remain relevant for modern life. If theology becomes formal, however, and invests its energies in theoretical and theological form, then it retains a method of asking questions of ultimate concern, and theology is then able to read other texts, in this case philosophical texts, under the pressure of existential or soteriological figurations of intensity and importance.

A formal theology does not have to abstract a positive theology from other kinds of texts, nor must it ask from a list of set questions such as "does the author believe in God?" A formal theology can be a critical theology, not just in the negative sense of the word, but in the sense of an interrogation of the main concepts, root metaphors, or aporetic formulations of a text, with a view toward raising questions of ultimacy without necessarily settling them, at least at the level of content. Kant himself allows transcendental theology validity only in its "negative employment," where "it serves as a permanent censor of our reason, in so far as the latter deals merely with pure ideas which, as such, allow of no criterion which is not transcendental" (A640/B668). A Kantian transcendental theology would interrogate the adequacy and applicability of ideas of reason.

IV

In order to amplify a constructive understanding of theology as formal, transcendental, and engaged with issues of ultimate concern, I want to suggest that a primary concern for theological reflection is the notion of orientation. The historian of religion Charles H. Long follows Tillich in defining religion as "orientation—orientation in the ultimate sense, that is, how one comes to terms with the ultimate significance of one's place in the world."[30] I would suggest that in a more specific Tillichean sense, religion in its existential sense refers to a basic orientation to reality. Theology, then, would represent the theoretical reflection which asks critical questions about the possibilities of orientation in general, as well as any particular orientation. Theologians and scholars desire in their writings to provide orientation to their readers, that is, to help them make sense of their world or their reality. Furthermore, most theologians want to minimize disorientation, in order to stress the harmony between reality and their specific interpretations of it. In a profound way, however, what is defined as religious represents that which challenges our orientations, and calls them into question in an unsettling way. In any event, absolute orientation is impossible, because otherwise orientation would simply be reality, while at the same time absolute disorientation is impossible, because then the question of orientation could not even arise. This book, however, attempts to value theological disorientation by taking seriously the Kantian sublime.

In his essay, "What is Orientation in Thinking?" Kant grapples explicitly with the issue of orientation, and suggests that the idea of God provides subjective orientation in thinking. Written in 1786, this piece represents Kant's intervention into the dispute between F.H. Jacobi and Moses Mendelssohn regarding the legitimacy and claims of faith and reason, respectively. Kant endorses the late Jewish philosopher, whose demise some contemporary intellectuals attributed to the unfair attacks of Jacobi and others, but in doing so he also modifies Mendelssohn's consistent rationalism. Although he affirms that "reason alone" is the "necessary means of orientation," Kant emphasizes that all of our rational concepts need certain "figurative notions" to make such concepts "suitable for use in the experiential world."[31] That is, rational concepts do not provide knowledge of themselves, but their actualization depends on "a felt need of reason" in order to provide orientation for human beings in thinking and living. There exists within reason, in a practical or heuristic sense, a "feeling of a need" which is a "subjective distinction" enabling judgment to occur.[32]

Reason cannot claim to provide knowledge of the world in any objective sense. Reason itself, however, according to Kant, is the only means of orienting human beings in the world, despite the arguments of fideists like Jacobi that God provides an objective center for orientation. Kant therefore concludes that reason provides subjective orientation based on a felt need for orientation to reality. Despite skepticism regarding the objective nature of the world,

> the right of the need of reason supervenes as a subjective ground for
> presupposing and accepting something which reason cannot presume

to know on objective grounds, and hence for orientating ourselves in thought—i.e., in the immeasurable space of the supra-sensory realm which we see as full of utter darkness—purely by means of the need of reason itself.[33]

From this premise Kant concludes that there is an unconditional need of reason to assume that God exists in the practical realm.

Kant uses the example of a person groping around in a dark room for direction; she is able to find her way around if she can locate a familiar object and orient herself practically by means of it. The disoriented person does not require a map of the room, only the ability to orient herself subjectively. Additionally, for an astronomer or stargazer, "in spite of all the objective data in the sky, I orientate myself geographically purely by means of a subjective distinction."[34] The importance of orientation is central for Kant, especially after he denies objective knowledge of things in themselves.

Kant is keenly aware of the dangers of disorientation. He describes the region of the supersensible as one of utter darkness, but claims that "in the darkness, I can orientate myself in a familiar room so long as I can touch any one object whose position I can remember."[35] In raising the question of disorientation, I am asking what happens if reason lacks knowledge of that absolute sun or Pole star by which it orients thinking.

Kant's philosophy becomes disoriented and disorienting most explicitly in the *Critique of Judgment*, in the Analytic of the Sublime. What are the risks for theology of attending to that disorientation, without too quickly attempting to orient oneself anew? If one brackets the sublime, the rest of Kantian philosophy can remain safe and secure, but what if the attention to the sublime disorients the rest of Kant's critical philosophy? And what if this disorientation is valued in theological thinking? In the first chapter of Genesis, "the earth was without form and void, with darkness over the face of the abyss, and a mighty wind that swept over the surface of the waters" (1: 2). The power and force of this image suggests that theology needs to be unsettled and unsettling. Even if shortly thereafter God provides light and orientation, theology can attend to the abyss of the deep and the disturbing of the waters that precedes the separation of light from darkness, day from night. What it loses in clarity and vision, a disorienting theology makes up for in power and intensity.

In his book *The Transparent Society*, Gianni Vattimo combines the Heideggerian notion of a blow with the idea of shock taken from Walter Benjamin in order to describe a work of art. For Heidegger a work of art delivers a blow to the observer, and Benjamin "describes the effect of cinema, as the art-form most characteristic of the age of technical reproduction, precisely in terms of shock."[36] Vattimo joins these two notions together in order to elaborate an aesthetic of disorientation. For Vattimo, "aesthetic experience is directed toward keeping the disorientation alive."[37] He criticizes Kant's aesthetics, because common sense, the *sensus communis*, or communal shared standards determine what can count as a beautiful work of art in what Kant claims to be a universal way. This unity of worldview is problematized by Vattimo, who argues that at present, "our experience of the beautiful in the recognition of models that make world and community is restricted to the moment when these worlds and communities present themselves explicitly as plural."[38] Vattimo neglects, however, the disorientation which comes about as a result of the Kantian sublime, despite Kant's intentions of restricting or containing it.[39] This disorientation of the senses in the sublime judgment not only pervades the aesthetic judgment of taste, or the beautiful, but it affects and makes tremble Kant's entire theoretical philosophical edifice.

A theology of the sublime concerns itself with the unrepresentable as such, and it locates itself not simply within aesthetic theory and art, but also at the heart of the *Critique of Pure Reason*, inhabiting our epistemology and technical knowledge. This study isolates a tension in Kant, a tension which drives his thinking, and which I am calling theological. This tension is formal in the sense that it no longer possesses a referent or an object, but refers to word as word, or the possibility of signification or representation, as I will show in Chapter Seven. The Kantian sublime not only represents an extreme case of disorientation, one that calls into question Kant's entire philosophical project, as we will see, but it also allows the possibility for orientation to occur. In this sense, the sublime could be figured as the religious *par excellence*.[40]

From a Kantian point of view, the sublime can be understood as that which disrupts orientation, in a manner akin to Rudolf Otto's "The Idea of the Holy." Otto, however, in calling the Holy numinous, refers to that which as an object shatters human capacity for representation externally, whereas a more genuinely Kantian understanding locates the unrepresentability within the very capacity or faculty to represent itself, as we will see in Chapter Five.[41] In terms of an understanding of religion, one could trace a trajectory from Kant through Schleiermacher to Otto and Tillich. Schleiermacher's "feeling of absolute dependence," Otto's "the Holy" and Tillich's "Depth of Reason" represent different formulations of the Kantian sublime. Here, religion understood as sublimity represents a profound sense of disorientation, which must also be considered in terms of orientation in general. Any manifestation of modern religiosity would then be thought under a particular mode of the Kantian sublime.

In a more general sense, Vattimo addresses the question of a relationship or orientation towards tradition in his book, *The End of Modernity*. In my attempts to articulate a radical theology, I may appear disparaging at times towards the traditions of classical theology and thinking, but this apparent hostility is in no way a dismissal of their importance. What, then, is the relation of a formal theology of disorientation, perhaps nearly unrecognizable to traditional theologies, to the traditions which have originated and nourished it?

For Vattimo, the relationship to the past for philosophy is one of *Andenken* and *Verwindung*. Borrowing both terms from Heidegger, Vattimo claims that *Andenken* is a rethinking, recollection, or recovery of the tradition or traditions at stake, while *Verwindung* represents a twisting free of the tradition, which does not thereby cease to be related to it. For Vattimo and Heidegger, the tradition at issue is the metaphysical tradition. For me, *Andenken* means that a theological investigation does not simply deal with the traditional objects or concepts of theology as they have been already determined and handed down, but in rethinking theological insights one must deal with the processes of understanding through experience which generate the theological conceptions in the first place. In this way, a theological thinking generates theology itself.

According to Vattimo, *Verwindung* is not *Überwindung*, or simple overcoming, but "it indicates a going-beyond which is both an acceptance and a deepening."[42] Vattimo shows that the German word *Verwindung* is also related to the notions of convalescence and resignation. For him, metaphysics "is not something which can be put aside . . . rather, it is something which stays in us as do the traces of an illness or a kind of pain to which we are resigned."[43] The metaphysical tradition must be "*verwunden*: recollected, distorted, accepted as a destiny,"[44] according to Vattimo. In an analogous way, theological thinking could conceive its relation to the traditions from which it has arisen—the metaphysical, the Christian, the Greek, the Jewish—as one of recollection, distortion, and acceptance as a destiny. This activity would not be a simple recovery or retrieval of any given tradition, which is impossible totally and purely, but as a radical theology would acknowledge its roots and rootedness in tradition and traditions,[45] and would also recognize the inevitability and necessity of deforming (in order to reform) that tradition or plurality of traditions. Vattimo usually leaves the word *Verwindung* untranslated, but where he tentatively offers a translation, he uses the word secularization, and it is this understanding of *Verwindung* as secularization to which I am appealing in my idea of a secular theology.[46]

The French theologian Gabriel Vahanian develops a theology which is fully secular and also utopian. Vahanian uses the concept of secularity in order to provide a region of orientation for theological thinking, and for Vahanian secular is *not* the opposite of sacred. His theological project takes place on a plane of immanence, because as a secular theology it presupposes a *saeculum*, or a shared world of human experience. Secular is not the opposite of sacred; rather, sacred and profane are opposites, and both are compatible with an understanding of culture in terms of secularity.[47]

The notion of utopia, however, serves to disorient any secure location for theological reflection. For Vahanian, theology is eschatological in that it deals not with the past but with the present and future. "If God reigns, it is neither over another world nor over (or beginning with) the end of the world, but over a world that is *other*."[48] Humanity is no-place (*ou-topos*), and this no-place is futurally oriented. Language is a technique, which when incarnated in a body becomes realized, and realizes a possibility which is utopian. Vahanian states that "it is the *religious* which will now assume the utopian function of language"[49] in a world which is more than profane and less than sacred, and this faith is envisioned as completely iconoclastic.

Vahanian provides a sophisticated theological meditation on these two terms, secularity and utopia. A biblical theologian, Vahanian sees secular Western culture developing out of a biblical ground. Whether or not one accepts his historical claims, his constructive theological project provides important resources to envision a contemporary theology which emphasizes his complex understandings of utopia and secularity. A contemporary secular theology is not opposed to manifestations of the sacred, but it affirms that expressions of transcendence must be at least indexed in terms of immanence, or in terms of a shared human world of experience. Such a theology also cannot have a secure place, whether in the Church or in the Academy. This utopian theology must call into question the adequacy of any and every place to express what it tries to express. A utopian theology is not simply a vision of a better or an ideal world in the future, that is to come, but rather a distention of the future in the present. This utopianism is futural in outlook or orientation, but it does not look literally to another world or to the end of this one. It is rather a dislocation of any simple location and the problematizing of any safe region from which to engage in theological thinking.

Conclusion

The vision of theology developed here is Kantian in form or methodology, to the extent that it is transcendental and critical. Kant's texts also represent a viable content or subject matter which can be interrogated theologically. As a significant representative of philosophical modernity, Kant's importance and influence testifies to the need to grapple theologically with the insights he expresses and the demands that he makes. A theological engagement with Kantian texts and ideas becomes relevant both within Kant's original framework as well as for the status of contemporary intellectual understanding.

This book represents the constitution of a problem in Kantian thought. This problem is important both for Kant and for us. The problem is not necessarily a new problem, for it takes place within the context of contemporary continental philosophy, but it is constituted anew. Quite simply, the problem is the disorientation introduced into the Kantian critical framework by and with the Analytic of the Sublime, and the effects of this disorientation, which cannot be contained within the *Critique of Judgment*. This problem, I am arguing, is the same problem which occurs in the *Critique of Pure Reason*, in the Transcendental Schematism. In fact, the problem is more important in the First Critique, but it is more visible in the Third Critique, which is why I am reading the *Critique of Judgment* back into the *Critique of Pure Reason*.

The constitution or location of a problem is not the same as a solution or resolution of a problem. Gilles Deleuze argues that the true task of philosophy lies in the constitution of problems rather than the solving of such problems. Once a framework is constructed in which a problem is defined as a problem, this determination constrains what can count as a solution. For Deleuze, "true freedom lies in a power to decide, to constitute problems themselves."[50] The stating of a problem as a problem involves more power and creativity than accepting a defined problem and attempting a solution. This stating of a problem, furthermore, "is not simply uncovering, it is inventing."[51] Deleuze emphasizes the value of creativity for philosophy, which consists in the creation of new concepts. This creativity is necessary for profound theological thinking, and the value of uncovering or constituting a theological problem in Kantian philosophy does not require or even presuppose a solution.

An appeal to Kantian philosophy allows an understanding of theology as a critical, formal, and transcendental theology which has no specific content given, but which interrogates, destabilizes, or disorients philosophical (and other kinds of) texts, including Kantian texts. Such a Kantian theology could be called a transcendental empiricism, which asks questions about the conditions of possibility (and impossibility) of experience. This experience should not be restricted to pure psychological experience or sense perception, which is the traditional understanding of empiricism. Experience, on the other hand, can be understood as divided, impure, mediated, and above all, as textual. An empiricism of textual experience asks transcendental questions about what constitutes a text as a text, and attends to the details or phenomena of that experience, but does not thereby close off any text from its interactions with other texts, other persons, and other worlds.

2 On modern sublimity
The challenge of Radical Orthodoxy

Introduction

The recent emergence of Cambridge Radical Orthodoxy, associated with John Milbank, Phillip Blond, Catherine Pickstock, and others, has injected a new vitality into theological thinking.[1] Radical Orthodoxy reads continental philosophy with sophistication, and attempts to fashion a constructive postmodern theology out of an encounter with thinkers such as Derrida, Deleuze, and Heidegger. Unfortunately, despite an incredible breadth and subtlety, as well as rhetorical suggestiveness, Radical Orthodoxy totalizes both philosophy and theology.

According to a simplified argument from the standpoint of Radical Orthodoxy, secular modernity is bad because it divorces reason from its ground in traditional faith and communal practice. Postmodern thinkers inspired by Nietzsche expose the limitations and aporias of modern secularity, but ultimately fail to move beyond them, because they are trapped within secular modernity's main assumptions. These assumptions must be jettisoned and replaced with genuine theological presuppositions in order to cure (post)modernity's discontents. The primary figure associated with secular reason, and the major opponent of Milbank's critique, is Kant.

Kant represents the height of secular modernity, before it gives way to Nietzsche's genealogical destruction of European reason and the Enlightenment tradition. The only way to avoid Nietzsche's relativism and nihilism, which lies at the heart of the later postmodern philosophers, is to eliminate the Enlightenment tradition and all of secular (that is, in Kantian terms, autonomous) reason, and base faith, politics, and society upon an entirely different foundation. This foundation is partially rediscovered and partially recreated, and relies on radical social thought, postmodern philosophers whose ideas have been taken up or sublated into a theological narrative, and an Anglican, Neo-Platonic reading of Thomas Aquinas.

Milbank draws upon Alasdair MacIntyre's philosophy, encapsulated in his Gifford lectures on *Three Rival Versions of Moral Enquiry*. According to MacIntyre, there are only three live options for philosophical ethics: encyclopedia (Kant), genealogy (Nietzsche) and tradition (Aristotle). MacIntyre stages a dramatic encounter in which genealogy deconstructs the claims of a universal, encyclopedic morality, but fails to provide a basis for its own moral and theoretical presuppositions. Genealogy, having finished off encyclopedia, basically implodes, leaving tradition as the sole alternative.

MacIntyre is a primary inspiration for Neo-Aristotelianism, which he articulates in his important book, *After Virtue*.[2] In *Three Rival Versions*, however, MacIntyre is more explicit about his constructive use of Aquinas to supplement and fulfil Aristotle in a way that takes into account Plato and Augustine on the one hand, and foresees and helps to solve the modern liberal existentialist dilemma, on the other. MacIntyre writes that Aquinas invokes Aristotle "against Aristotle in the interests of scripture and of Augustine, not because Aquinas was rejecting Aristotelianism, but because he was trying to be a better Aristotelian than Aristotle."[3] Furthermore, despite his being a precursor to a Hobbesian "discovery of human inability and resourcelessness to live by the natural law and to achieve the excellence of the virtues," which "points forward to a kind of existential despair which was completely unknown in the ancient world," Aquinas manages to turn a negative into a positive. For Aquinas, "it is in fact this discovery of willful evil which makes the achievement of the human end possible," because "the acknowledgment by oneself of radical defect is a necessary condition for one's reception of the virtues of faith, hope and charity."[4] MacIntyre's moral theory provides an important source and context for Milbank's thought.

I

In his magisterial work, *Theology and Social Theory*, Milbank indicts modern secular reason, condemning all of modern thought as autonomous and therefore necessarily implicated in violence. Secular modernity is a wrenching away from a harmonious tradition, and the resulting modern theory and practice is blamed for all of the violence and suffering of contemporary human beings. Such modern secularity reenacts a presupposition of pagan antiquity: "there emerges a hidden thread of continuity between antique reason and modern, secular reason. This thread of continuity is the theme of original violence."[5]

Milbank associates violence with antique and modern reason, and dissociates violence from Christianity. He claims to "show that from the outset the secular is complicit with an 'ontology of violence,' a reading of the world which assumes the priority of force and tells how this force is best managed and confined by a counter-force." On the other hand, Christianity "recognizes no original violence. It construes the infinite not as chaos, but as a harmonic peace which is yet beyond the circumscribing power of any totalizing reason."[6] This central assertion is problematic, both idealistically and empirically or historically. The analysis of the complicity of liberal European modernity with technical power, intrinsic violence and control is detailed and profound, although it follows generally Foucauldian lines. However, this political critique idealizes premodern Christian society and its concomitant violence, which it sees as extrinsic or accidental rather than necessary. Not only many social theorists, but also significant contemporary theologians, including Gabriel Vahanian and Thomas J.J. Altizer, stress the continuity of Christianity and European modernity. Does modern European civilization develop out of medieval European society, or does it come about as the result of an absolute break or fall? This question is in some way Hegelian, because Hegel would assert that even if modernity is a reversal of premodern Christian society, modernity is nevertheless intrinsically related to Christianity, at least dialectically.

So, it may not be possible to assert such neat historical divisions. Another difficult question is the relation of the violence of the twentieth century to the agenda of the Enlightenment, that is, whether World War II and the Holocaust represent a tragic betrayal or horrifying fulfillment of basic Enlightenment ideals.[7] In earlier time periods, Milbank is at pains to separate an authentic Christianity from other social and intellectual phenomena, primarily the profound influence of Neo-Platonism on early Christian theology and mysticism. For instance, in a critical essay, Douglas Hedley, a Cambridge Platonist, charges:

> The obvious source of Augustine's or Gregory of Nyssa's metaphysics, however, is not, of course, Plato or Aristotle, but late antique Platonism. This has been well established since the early part of the twentieth century, but it is a fact that Milbank tends to ignore—and with good reason. The prominence of Neoplatonic metaphysical tenets in the Church fathers militates against Milbank's own philosophy–theology distinction.[8]

Finally, what about violence perpetuated by Christianity? Milbank denies that violence is intrinsic to Christianity, and dissociates violence committed by or in the name of Christianity as secondary or accidental. This claim is suspect for at least three reasons:

1   One of the major influences upon the development of autonomous reason and the Enlightenment is the effect of the Protestant and Catholic Reformations and the wars of religion. The incredible violence unleashed across Europe for over a century, from the mid-1500s until the

Treaty of Westphalia which ended the Thirty Years War in 1648, was generated and sustained by Christian conflicts. Certainly, "secular" political considerations of wealth and power played a tremendous role, but the reaction of European intelligentsia to this bloodshed was to seek an alternative basis for faith. The problem was that revelation was so individualistic once the power of the Roman Catholic Church was shaken by Luther's success, that no higher or neutral arbiter could mediate claims of faith and salvation. In addition, scripture could be read and interpreted in many different ways, and no consensus or authority existed to enforce an orthodox reading. The resulting autonomy of reason was an attempt to appeal to a universal basis to resolve competing claims of faith and morals. In his book *Cosmopolis*, Stephen Toulmin shows how these events and concerns influenced Descartes' *Meditations*.[9] The aftermath of the wars of religion also prompted the efforts to develop and promote toleration, often against powerful religious and political interests who aligned force with power.

2   Christianity defines itself in opposition to Judaism, even though it bases its rejection of Judaism on Jewish rejection of Christ as the Messiah, and also at times upon fabricated claims that the Jews were responsible for putting Jesus to death. The result of the Christian rejection of Judaism is an interpretation of the destruction of the Jewish Temple in Jerusalem during the first Jewish Revolt as a judgment of God upon the Jews, in addition to an attempt to whitewash Roman tyranny and political power.[10] This uneasy relationship with Judaism has resulted in an intrinsic and pervasive theological anti-Judaism which does not seem to fit into Milbank's picture of peace and harmony.[11] Tragically, this anti-Judaism has also historically expressed itself as a virulent anti-semitism, and resulted in considerable violence during many periods of Christian history. The acknowledgment of Christian complicity in medieval ghettos and modern pogroms does not even touch on the question of Christian complicity in the Holocaust, which is a much-discussed and disputed issue.[12]

3   For many Christians, the central symbol of their religion is the cross, and the central event is the crucifixion of Jesus Christ. By idealizing Christian theology and practice, Milbank tends to downplay the significance of the cross, which is a symbol of violence, even if it ultimately represents the overcoming of violence and death. Here an originary violence exists at the heart of Christianity, which can be alleviated but not overcome without seriously distorting Christian identity. In his *Commentary on Galatians*, Luther explains how the grace of God in Christ is a law applied to the law. The crucifixion and death of Christ represent the death of law and death, in a doubling of death, or a negation of negation which brings about (eternal) life. Here Luther

follows and elaborates on a Pauline theology, which is eerily similar to Milbank's characterization of modern reason. Luther writes that "in the Scriptures, and especially in Paul, the law is set against the law, sin against sin, death against death." Here violence is internal to the process and force can only be constrained by a counter-force, which converts and overcomes the original force: "So death killeth death: but this killing death is life itself."[13]

Milbank's broad theological claims can be troubled historically. Violence may threaten Christianity from the inside, as well as result from its practical enforcement. What about his specific criticisms of Kant, however, and his association of Kantian sublimity with secular modernity and its discontents? Why is Kant the fundamental enemy of Radical Orthodoxy?

II

What is a transcendental argument? How can transcendental and theological notions be compared and distinguished? According to John Milbank, Kantian transcendental arguments are "metaphysically dogmatic" rather than an "innocent, descriptive account of our finitude, or the permanent limits of our human being."[14] Milbank claims that by circumscribing the limits of finite, phenomenal experience, Kant is more dogmatic than Thomas Aquinas, who leaves open the limits of human knowing for the possibility of analogical participation in divine being. On the one hand, I also critique Kant's claims regarding phenomenal experience, and suggest from within that his realm of appearances cannot be safeguarded from the critical energy he has unleashed regarding transcendent objects of experience. On the other hand, one can read Kantian transcendental arguments (as well as other transcendental arguments) as more heuristic and less rigid, along the lines of what Rodolphe Gasché (referring to Derrida) calls "quasi-transcendental."[15] Milbank attempts to sharpen the choice between a postmodern theology of linguistic participation in divine creation and resurrection and a nihilistic postmodernism identified with Nietzsche and Derrida. He writes: "There is then no liberal enclave in which one can shelter from 'mystical nihilism.' The real cultural issue lies between this nihilism and theology."[16] To refuse a forced choice between nihilism and faith is to be labeled a nihilist, although neither Nietzsche nor Derrida would describe themselves in this way. I understand theology in a more Tillichean way, as the knife edge between faith and doubt embodied in a radical and unsettling interrogation of the limits of experience.

The metaphorical nature of transcendental questions or conditions must be stressed. They represent the limits of what can be seen and said and known right now, but these limits are not fixed or permanent (which is not to say that knowledge or thinking takes the form of a progression or enlargement, but rather indicates the flux of thought and ideas). Space and time represent transcendental conditions of sensible intuition for Kant, and these claims should be taken seriously, but that does not mean that they should not be troubled, or that other transcendental conditions of intuition cannot be envisioned or inserted, such as language. In fact, Milbank argues that language mediates reality in a transcendental way.[17] The fact that one cannot be certain regarding the status of transcendental or *a priori* claims, however, does not prevent using them as tools to ask theological questions. And these theological questions cut into and unsettle experience in such a way that they cause disorientation, whereas Milbank, who professes to perform a "task of redeeming estrangement," ends up with an all-too-comforting orthodoxy.[18] It is a serious and important question Milbank raises, whether the delineation of the limits of experience prescribes and proscribes what can count as an experience in a way that dismisses experiences which do not take that form, but to be aware of such a concern is not to sweepingly dismiss a complex Kantian transcendentality.

Despite his dismissal of Kant from a position of relevance for postmodern theology, Milbank recognizes the importance of the aesthetic of the sublime for Kant's philosophical project. "Kant's entire philosophy," Milbank writes, "is in a sense an aesthetic of the sublime in which one is brought up against the margin of organized, formal, 'beautiful' experience, and at this margin becomes overwhelmed by the intimation of the materially formless, and infinitely total."[19] To a great extent, this book will confirm Milbank's insight, but in a far more ambivalent and powerful way than Milbank's simple rejection of modern sublimity. Milbank recoils from the theological implications of this insight because he is concerned that a "theology of right" becomes an empty formalism or procedure in which one is anonymous before the moral law, as opposed to a theology of the good which possesses material content. Milbank asserts that contemporary thinking calls into question the form–content distinction, but I do not thereby want to dismiss the theological significance of a preoccupation with form, even if no pure form exists abstracted from all material, empirical experience (and even Kant knows this). Sometimes to push an idea to its limits yields more insight than a corrective, common-sense balance. So this reading concerns itself with form, especially theological form, or theology as form, but always at the moment when it is threatened by the formlessness or disorientation which marks the sublime. I will suggest that this very formlessness is what allows form or orientation in the first place, most importantly in the schematism of the First Critique. Milbank rejects the formlessness which characterizes the sublime in order to return to a pure form of Thomistic or Platonic knowing which manifests the transcendent without any disorientation or negativity.

III

A secular postmodern theological thinking opposes the simple rejection of secular modernity undertaken by contemporary Radical Orthodoxy. As I have suggested, Radical Orthodoxy focuses on Kantian sublimity in order to demonstrate the failures of European modernity in its universalist pretensions. Postmodern philosophers such as Derrida, Deleuze, and Lyotard demonstrate the aporias of modern secular philosophy by deconstructing its foundational claims. These postmodern philosophers themselves must be overcome, however, because by accepting the premises of secularity and modernity, they cannot prevent their philosophies from resulting in nihilism.

In *Post-Secular Philosophy*, Phillip Blond repeats Milbank's basic argument, claiming that secular modernity establishes itself by denying the transcendent. Blond calls this denial sublime, because although "a self-sufficient finitude denies itself any relation with infinity," it cannot avoid being troubled by what it has exorcised. Blond claims that since Kant confines the sublime within the limits of reason and rationality, and thus denies any transcendence, "the peculiar though understandable result of all this is that God becomes both unknowable and yet deeply feared" as an external object which cannot be accessed by human reason.[20] For Blond, "a self-sufficient finitude denies itself any relationship with infinity," but this denial produces anxiety, which gives rise to postmodern critiques of the limits of immanent experience, which do not however achieve a breakthrough to transcendence.[21] To combat this negativity, Blond calls for an overcoming of modern sublimity via a renewal of the perception of transcendence. Only a radical orthodoxy which is truly a postmodern theology can call into question the claims of modern secularity in the first place, and can envision a philosophy which would once again play handmaiden to theology. This vision recalls the perfection of a medieval Thomistic synthesis in which God is understood as both powerful and beneficent, and looks forward to an understanding of humanity which is approached through the nobility of its possibility rather than the messy negativity of its actuality, repeating themes from MacIntyre and Milbank.

One of the most important essays in *Post-Secular Philosophy* seemingly reinforces the claims of Blond and Radical Orthodoxy, but it also provides a basis for seriously critiquing its reading of the Kantian sublime. In his essay, "Descartes and Ontotheology," Jean-Luc Marion describes how in the *Meditations* Descartes separates the *cogito* as thinking being from God understood as power or causality. Prior to this paradigmatic moment which instantiates modernity, God was represented by scholastic philosophy and theology as both thinking intelligibility and as the source of power which causes all effects in and of the world. Descartes reformulates thinking being in terms of human subjectivity, which means that God is excluded from intelligible subjectivity. Since Descartes recognizes a limit to his own power of subjectivity, God becomes defined as that limit, or the power of an unthinking causality external to the subject. "God does not so much cogitate as He cannot cogitate," writes Marion. "The exercise of the *cogitatio* neither reaches Him [sic] nor defines Him as much as does the exercise of power."[22]

God understood as power is both uncomprehending—God cannot be thought of as thinking—and incomprehensible. Therefore God is experienced in modernity by human subjectivity as sublime. A central project of postmodern theologians such as Marion and Milbank is to reconceptualize divinity as *cogitatio*, thereby overcoming modernity. In this context, Kant represents a key opponent, because the Kantian sublime, understood in the light of postmodern and poststructuralist critiques, still envisions God as incomprehensible power, which can only be a source of incomprehension and fear.

Despite their recognition that the Kantian sublime refers to the faculties of human reason, rather than external objects, both Milbank and Blond fail to grasp the radicality of Kant's juxtaposition. Many thinkers misunderstand the sublime because they think that it refers to an enormous or powerful object, rather than to the subject's conflict of faculties in perceiving such an object. Although Milbank and Blond realize that the sublime involves processes of the mind, they tend to characterize God as the object which results from this process, or that which is referred to in conjunction with this process, who can only be a source of incomprehension and fear. Marion demonstrates that after Descartes, God becomes an incomprehensible source of fear because God is external to the subject (an object). As I will demonstrate in this study, however, Kant relocates God (or the sublime) as internal to subjectivity, as that which makes the subject possible as a subject. Subjectivity is no more intelligible than God, and the ground of subjectivity experienced as fear and terror is madness.

Following Kant, God is not an object of experience, transcendent or otherwise. The sublime takes place at the heart of the subject, in the transcendental imagination which makes knowledge of an object possible in the first place, which represents the convergence of what Descartes separated, that is, *cogito* and power. If the sublime is identified with God (or divine power), however tentatively, then God powerfully reappears within subjectivity, shattering it from inside, as the force of the negative imagination. This conclusion is what my theological reading of the Kantian critiques will demonstrate. This reading places Kant in theoretical continuity with Descartes, according to Marion's reading, but here Kant reunites what Descartes had put asunder. God becomes internal to the process of human thinking and representation, rather than external as a locus of transcendent power and terrifying might. Despite Kant's stated claims that God belongs solely in the moral sphere as a practical idea, the logic of

Kantian thought in the First and Third Critiques identifies a thinking of divinity with the analytic of the sublime, which is the same logic that appears in the transcendental imagination or Schematism.

The location of the sublime at the heart of the subject in a radically decentering manner distorts Radical Orthodoxy's logic of modern sublimity as merely an external object which is the source of incomprehension and fear. Rather, this source of incomprehension and fear which I am isolating in terms of the negative power of imagination makes the subject what it is. This fundamental insight challenges a phenomenological theological project which aims to purify thinking and subjectivity of its sublimity.[23] Sublimity, as I will show, constitutes the modern or post-Kantian subject, and the implications of such a subject are deeply theological.

IV

This reunion of a thinking and power associated traditionally with God at a level internal to human representation is not a happy marriage, however, but attests to a fissuring of that representation. Radical Orthodoxy cannot admit of any negativity in its thinking of either humanity or divinity. This insistence on excluding all negativity becomes a totalizing blind spot, because every expression of ambiguity, finitude or suffering must be wished away by an insistence upon the magnificence of God which implies a concomitant emphasis on the positivity of human possibility.

Radical Orthodoxy's insistence that any theology must be a positive theology hinges on its understanding of aesthetics, which is inspired by the work of Hans Urs von Balthasar. In the Introduction to Volume II of *The Glory of the Lord*, Balthasar explains that the purpose of his work is to stress the "ineffable beauty" that characterizes the Christian interpretation of the "revelation of the living God."[24] God must be understood, however excessively, in analogy with worldly beauty. Balthasar builds upon the positive aesthetics of the later Barth of the *Church Dogmatics* in order to emphasize the free self-revelation of God in which each mystical "*via negativa . . .* stands in the service of a positive way." The logic of beauty is a logic of form, the form of self-revelation of God, world, and humanity from out of the "dazzling darkness of divine beauty:"

> It is not that which remains inaccessible when God has manifested himself in Christ; rather it is on the contrary the splendour which breaks forth from this love of God which gives itself without remainder and is poured forth in the form of worldly powerlessness: the superabundant power of the light and meaning of love, as it shines forth in the form, causes it to become necessarily a form of veiling— just because it reveals that which is utmost, the ineffable.[25]

Radical Orthodoxy desires to hold onto this mystery of God, which is necessarily veiled and veiling, and yet at the same time to follow von Balthasar and insist on the ultimately positive and beautiful form of this divine manifestation. Just as von Balthasar associates what is distinctively Christian in earlier theologians with a positive aesthetics of beauty, Radical Orthodoxy transmutes an ethical concern with violence explicit in Milbank's *Theology and Social Theory* into an insistence on beauty at the expense of the sublime. Von Balthasar, however, holds onto a notion of the sublime which functions in the service of beauty, which is the reverse of Kant's structure in the Third Critique where beauty ultimately serves the ends of the moral sublime. For von Balthasar, "everything of beauty found in the world . . . is drawn up into a relationship to this inexhaustible standard, where the living God of love is glorified as he pours out his limitless love for the creature kenotically into the void which is empty of himself."[26] Von Balthasar assembles an impressive theological aesthetics for the sake of a theological dramatics which stages the beauty of the form in narrative drama. "If God presents himself in the world, then there lies in that an act of the most sublime freedom," he writes.[27] The sublime freedom of God is guaranteed by its analogy with a worldly beauty that also preserves goodness and truth.

Von Balthasar's sublime beauty would function as a pre- or postmodern antithesis to the Kantian modern sublime, according to the logic of Radical Orthodoxy. I will show how the Kantian sublime fundamentally involves a negative aesthetics, and leads to a breaking or at least stretching of beautiful form. This conclusion may not be desirable for human theological concerns about the beauty, goodness, and truth of God, but the Kantian sublime may be integral to modern and contemporary human experience. This experience may be deemed undesirable, but it may not be simply wished away, and furthermore it may be much more complex than the totalizing critique of Radical Orthodoxy suggests.

In *Theology and Social Theory*, Milbank values Deleuze's ontology of difference, but only insofar as it is shorn of its Nietzschean and Kantian presuppositions. "In the case of Deleuze," Milbank writes, "his non-dialectical, 'positive' version of difference seems only to issue in nihilism because of lingering Kantian assumptions and sheer cultural bias."[28] The cultural bias is a bias against Christianity and its social forms which Milbank wants to valorize, and in later chapters I will demonstrate the extent to which Deleuze remains deeply implicated in Kantian thinking. According to Milbank, Deleuze's differential logic opens up possibilities for theology, but his positive notion of ontological difference instantiates an agonistic conflict based on Nietzsche and Kant.

Milbank desires a theology of difference, but one based on accord rather than discord. Milbank's hatred of discord is so profound that he links any discord necessarily to violence, even if such discord functions in the service of a higher accord. Differences must be harmonious and never conflictual—"thinking an infinite differentiation that is also a harmony: this is what grounds the reconciliation of difference with virtue."[29] This harmonious infinite differentiation is Deleuzian in a way, but Milbank curbs the chaotic aspect of Deleuze's work and introduces a teleology which orders the differences. Harmony cannot exist without teleological order. Order makes up the basis of beauty and truth, a Christian truth which is "participation of the beautiful in the beauty of God."[30] This demand may work at the level of a demand, but the question is whether such teleology is credible at the level of reality and human experience, despite our need for it to be so.

For Milbank, Christianity appeals to the Trinity as a mythos that ensures order and harmony, which corrects Deleuze's ancient myth of "violent, agonistic difference."[31] On the one hand, serious questions can be raised about Milbank's reading of Deleuze, because order and harmony function in a minimalistic way to allow creativity and vitality, and Deleuze never sees differences as intrinsically oppositional. In the conclusion to *What is Philosophy?* Deleuze and Guattari explore the confrontation between the brain and chaos, but assert: "We require just a little order to protect us from chaos."[32]

On the other hand, Deleuze disqualifies an external teleology which overdetermines the ordering of events, which is what Milbank requires of the Triune God. Milbank wants a Deleuze without the swerve, that is, the uncertainty which threatens to plunge thinking into dumbness and chaos at any moment; and yet this swerve is, for Deleuze, the condition of fruitful thinking. Milbank would disallow placing any negative conditions on what thinking is and can be, although he also places his own positive conditions and orthodox framework upon human social and religious experience. He is correct that there is no neutral frame or standpoint from which to ask theological questions—we ask them from where we are, and we deny or affirm specific answers and particular valuations based on our own guilt and innocence. Milbank works against a certain totalizing viewpoint, that of autonomous modern reason, and yet his opposition forces him to articulate a totalizing view of his own, that of a Radical Orthodoxy which ends up looking much more orthodox than radical, as Douglas Hedley concludes:

> Far from being very radical, Milbank's theology conforms to the currents of theological fashion in an exemplary manner. The titles of this dominant tendency vary somewhat: "post-liberal," "Radical Orthodoxy," "confessional," and so forth, but the result is the same. Theology should be seen as Church dogmatics.[33]

V

Milbank is constrained to attack and refute the theories of Deleuze and Derrida, at the same time as he makes use of some of their insights. In this book I use the philosophies of Deleuze and Derrida in a complementary way to interrogate and deepen Kantian thinking in a manner which suggests important implications for theology. Derrida's philosophical project can be broadly regarded as a critique of metaphysical claims to self-presence, which is ultimately an "onto-theological" claim. I read Derrida in the lineage of a Kantian critique of metaphysics, despite Derrida's concern at times to differentiate himself from Kant.[34] Derrida's deconstructive critique, however, also pressures and distorts Kant's critical aims, even as it helps translate and illuminate them. In the service of his deconstructive project, Derrida continually appeals to literary figures such as Mallarmé, Melville, Genet and Shakespeare in order to expose philosophy to an outside or an other, which calls its most powerful claims and demands into question. I want to suggest that, in an analogous way, for the discourse of theology, philosophy provides such an external role.

Many theologians are anxious to dissociate themselves from philosophical methods and results, presuming that philosophy has to do with human and secular concerns while theology has to do with divine ones. Theology is particularly anxious, however, because theological writing usually assumes a philosophical or at least logical form. Many theologians can only safely approach philosophical thinking on the condition that it can be subsumed or sublated (in an Hegelian *Aufhebung*) by theology. Thus John Milbank argues that "only theology overcomes metaphysics," and therefore one must "*evacuate* all philosophy, leaving it merely as the empty science of formally possible perspectives and barren *aporias.*"[35] In a similar move (although Milbank is critical of its success), Jean-Luc Marion wants to think God beyond the constraints of the category of being and preceding the Heideggerian ontological difference between being and beings, in *God Without Being: Hors-Texte*. The subtitle of this book, which is not reproduced on the cover of the English version, makes Derrida's famous phrase, "*il n'y a pas de hors-texte*" (literally, "there is no *hors-texte*," there is no God without, outside of, or uncontaminated by being), interestingly relevant.[36]

Such an evacuation of philosophy is then made the condition of authentic theologizing. What is striking, given this claim, is that in his essay, "The Linguistic Turn as a Theological Turn," Milbank identifies the culmination of Christian orthodox theology with "the theologically informed philosophy of lay thinkers" of the eighteenth century such as Berkeley, Vico, and J.G. Hamann.[37] In a similar way, Marion, in *Reduction and Givenness*, attempts to establish a pure phenomenology of givenness which would provide support for a theology of donation via an authentic reread-ing of Husserl and Heidegger.[38]

Theological claims are in some ways the most grandiose, because they are statements concerning (and constitutive of) the divine. Finite humans, however, cannot simply, immediately, or adequately speak or write the divine, which is why Milbank and others want to overcome human finitude as a limit. In Kantian terms, God as the condition for the possibility of the totality of experience cannot be an object of experience. Karl Barth presents the situation as one of obligation and impossibility:

> As ministers [read theologians] we ought to speak of God. We are human, however, and so cannot speak of God. We ought therefore to recognize both our obligation and our inability and by that very recog-nition give God the glory. This is our perplexity. The rest of our task fades into insignificance in comparison.[39]

Since no immediate knowledge of God can be possessed, or knowledge of the world by means of what Kant calls intellectual intuition, philosophical language must be resorted to in order to attempt to think about the divine. Philosophy as an outside or other to theology subverts its totalizing claims and provides what Kant calls a "transcendental critique of theology." Theology stands in need of such critique because it claims to know or possess (whether discursively or intuitively) the truth which it invokes or to which it points. This demand to think or speak the ultimate cannot be avoided, but it also cannot be approached directly in a non-metaphorical way. Furthermore, any theological claim must be subject to deconstruction or else it becomes guilty of what Tillich calls idolatry.[40] The necessary distance or caesura between theology and what it attempts to represent is necessarily philosophical, that is, secular and immanent, rather than transcendent.

Tillich argues, in *Biblical Religion and the Search for Ultimate Reality*, that "there is no pure revelation." Since "wherever the divine is manifest, it is manifest in 'flesh,'" what Tillich calls biblical religion must be con-fronted with philosophy.[41] Tillich charges that "it is infuriating to see how biblical theologians . . . use most of the terms created by the toil of phi-losophers and the ingenuity of the speculative mind and then dismiss, with cheap denunciations, the work from which their language has been im-mensely enriched."[42] For theologians to use philosophical distinctions and categories in their work and then to impugn philosophy itself as corrupt and sinful is to a certain extent intellectually weak and smugly self-serving.

I also want to raise the question, in a Tillichean vein, whether the term theology can continue to be restricted to Christian theology (it is originally a Greek term), or even Western religions. What would a Buddhist theology, understood as the reflective self-expression of a religion by its adherents, look like? Sensitive intellectuals concerned that the term theology necessarily connotes Western imperialism should also note that the word religion is originally a Western term applied to non-Western phenomena in a way that is no less problematic.[43] While what is understood as religion can never simply be accepted as given, and the bounds or limits must constantly be redefined, Kantian philosophy here provides impetus and occasion to reconceive and reconsider the tasks and the limits of theological reflection.

Conclusion

The engagement with Radical Orthodoxy provides a critical encounter in which to fashion a truly radical theological thinking. This encounter isolates the centrality of the Kantian sublime for the critical thought of Radical Orthodoxy, which contrasts with the reading developed here. Preparatory to directly engaging the Kantian texts of the First and Third Critiques, in the following chapter I will introduce Heidegger's and Lyotard's interpretations of Kant which set the stage for rereading Kant along with Derrida and Deleuze.

3 Ontology and linguistics
Heidegger and Lyotard

Introduction

This chapter examines the interpretations of Kant by Martin Heidegger and Jean-François Lyotard, in order to provide a context and a framework for the reading of Kant which is developed later in the book. Each thinker produces an original work of philosophy which is influenced by Kant, and then each writes an important interpretation of Kantian critical philosophy. Heidegger writes *Being and Time*, and follows it with *Kant and the Problem of Metaphysics*; Lyotard writes *The Differend* and later *Lessons on the Analytic of the Sublime*.[1] Heidegger provides important tools or categories for continental philosophical interpretation of Kant: subjectivity, imagination, temporality, and schematism. Heidegger reinterprets the *Critique of Pure Reason* in a forceful way that opposes Neo-Kantian idealism and its focus upon the *Critique of Practical Reason*. Lyotard reinterprets the *Critique of Judgment* along Heideggerian lines, and makes his reading of the Third Critique the model for knowing in his philosophy. One way to summarize their respective interpretations would be to say that Heidegger ontologizes Kant, whereas Lyotard linguicizes Kant. This claim should become clear during the course of the chapter.

I

How can it be claimed that Heidegger ontologizes Kant, when in the *Critique of Pure Reason* Kant argues that "the proud name of Ontology ... must, therefore, give place to the modest title of a mere Analytic of pure understanding" (A247/B303)? For Kant, ontology represents human ability to know things as they are in themselves. By restricting knowledge to appearances, and to the transcendental conditions for our knowledge of appearances, Kant reduces human transcendental knowledge to the application of the categories of pure understanding. What Heidegger ontologizes is that process or activity of understanding, by tying it to *Dasein*, or the being of that entity that asks the question of being. Kant's "Copernican revolution" consists in turning away from objects in themselves toward subjective processes of human knowledge or understanding. Heidegger ontologizes that subjective process of understanding, and he shows how it takes place existentially.

In *Being and Time*, Heidegger asks what being is, apart from its occurrence in particular beings. He claims that what distinguishes the human being is her ability to ask questions about the meaning of being. We can only get at the meaning of being in itself through the being which we are and with which we are concerned. Heidegger concludes that the essence or being of the human being, or *Dasein*, is care. Care means concern for its own being on the part of *Dasein*, which also implies care for the being of others. Heidegger goes on to suggest that this understanding of care is temporal, because human beings are always finite, and exist in a state of being-towards-death. If humans did not foresee the future nonexistence of their own being, they could not take it up as a matter of concern. This notion of care can be seen as individualistic, but Heidegger qualifies this understanding in an important way when he suggests that the being of *Dasein* cannot be separated from "Being-with Others," or *Mit-sein*. Ultimately, Heidegger concludes that *"Dasein's* Being is Being-with (*Mit-sein*)."[2] In defining "temporality as the ontological meaning of care," Heidegger wants to connect being and time on the level of finite human existence, or existential being in the world.[3]

How is this project of Heidegger's an interpretation of Kant? Kant not only claims that all knowledge begins with experience (B1), but also prohibits any knowledge which does not apply to sensory experience. The First Critique is engaged in working out the transcendental or *a priori* conditions by which knowledge of an object is possible. This identification of transcendental conditions is in some ways a method of abstraction, but Kant stresses that these conditions only apply to empirical sense experience. Any claim to transcendent knowledge of objects which transcend sense experience is a dialectical illusion which Kant attempts to expose and deny in the second half of the *Critique of Pure Reason*.[4] By treating the transcendental conditions of experience, Kant is, from Heidegger's point of view, always oriented toward human being-in-the-world. Kant distinguishes, then, between transcendental and empirical knowledge. Heidegger uses the terms "ontological" and "ontic" to make a similar distinction. Ontic knowledge refers to knowledge of particular beings, or the empirical appearances of experiences as they appear to us, while ontological knowledge refers to knowledge of the being of beings, or the transcendental conditions by which any appearance can be an experience for us. Charles M. Sherover claims that Heidegger reformulates Kantian transcendental knowledge into "the term 'ontological knowledge,' i.e., the knowledge of the non-experiential (or Kantian *a priori* transcendental) grounds for any particular thing to be capable of being known to us. Similarly, just as Kant regarded any empirical knowledge as a particular bit of information . . . so Heidegger has rendered this experiential particularity by the word 'ontic'."[5] In *Being and Time*, Heidegger conducts an ontological inquiry into the conditions of ontic knowledge and experience in terms of human (*Dasein*) being-in-the-world. As Sherover writes, "*Being and Time* can be regarded as providing the ontological grounding of the general nature of Kantian epistemology."[6]

In *Kant and the Problem of Metaphysics*, Heidegger claims that his task is to interpret "Kant's *Critique of Pure Reason* as a laying of the ground for metaphysics and thus of placing the problem of metaphysics before us as a fundamental ontology."[7] This laying of foundations is for Heidegger an ontological grounding, because it provides the conditions for the possibility of metaphysical thinking. He engages the heart of the First Critique directly, and emphasizes the importance of the pure productive power of imagination. In the *Critique of Pure Reason*, the transcendental imagination mediates between sensory intuitions and the categories or pure concepts of the understanding. One of Kant's most controversial moves is his division of human knowing into intuitions of sense and concepts of understanding. Sense intuitions intuit a manifold, but as a completely passive faculty, sensibility lacks any ability to unify them into a coherent representation or determinate object of knowledge. The understanding is an active faculty that unifies the manifold of sense intuitions into objective concepts, thereby providing knowledge. But a bifurcation between sensibility and understanding leaves Kant with a profound and difficult need to close the gap. That is, how are the sensible intuitions related to the categories or concepts of the understanding, or how does knowledge arise in this way? This explanation is the task of the Transcendental Deduction of the Categories, which is considered by scholars to be the most difficult and complex part of the First Critique, and which was almost completely rewritten by Kant himself in the second edition of the Critique.[8]

According to Heidegger, imagination occupies a central place as a mediating faculty between sensibility and understanding. For Kant, "we must assume a pure transcendental synthesis of imagination as conditioning the very possibility of all experience" insofar as it makes possible the "reproducibility of appearances" (A102). Imagination mediates the sensory intuitions of the manifold to the unifying categories or pure concepts of the understanding in what Kant calls a synthesis. This central role in the Transcendental Deduction suggests that imagination is more significant than most analytic interpreters of Kant generally acknowledge.

Kant splits synthesis into three parts, corresponding to the three capacities or faculties of the human mind: sensibility, imagination, and understanding. As H.J. Paton points out, this synthesis consists of:

(1) a synthesis of the *apprehension* of ideas, as modifications of the mind in intuition; (2) a synthesis of the *reproduction* of ideas in imagination; and (3) a synthesis of their *recognition* in the concept.[9]

Even though Kant splits the activity of synthesis into three parts, the imagination still holds the middle or central role, and Kant elsewhere claims that "synthesis in general" is the "mere result of the power of imagination" (A78/B103).

Heidegger notes that for Kant, "all synthesis is brought about from the power of imagination," and this power of imagination to synthesize is the activity which brings about knowledge, that is, the fusion of sensible intuitions and conceptual categories.[10] For Heidegger,

> the transcendental power of imagination is not just an external bond which fastens together two ends. It is originally unifying, i.e., as a particular faculty it forms the unity of both of the others, which themselves have an essential structural relatedness to it.[11]

Heidegger argues that the faculty or capacity of imagination is given more independence and importance in the first edition of the First Critique, but that Kant shrinks back from the disturbing power of imagination in the second edition, because it had threatened to swallow both understanding and intuition. Citing Kant's statement that "there are two stems of human knowledge, namely, sensibility and understanding, which perhaps spring forth from a common, but to us unknown, root" (A15/B29), Heidegger suggests that the transcendental power of imagination is the root of both stems.[12] In the second edition of the *Critique of Pure Reason*, the independent faculty of imagination with all of its productive power of synthesis, is collapsed into the faculty of understanding. Heidegger claims that "Kant did not carry through with the more original interpretation of the transcendental power of imagination . . . On the contrary: Kant shrank back from this unknown root."[13]

Heidegger highlights the importance of the transcendental imagination in the First Critique. Kant fears the power of imagination because it threatens the objectivity he has fought so hard to establish, at the cost of limiting our knowledge to things as they appear to us. How does this treatment of imagination relate to temporality and subjectivity, however? Heidegger teases out the close connection between imagination and apperception, which provides the unity of self-consciousness for Kant, as well as the connection between the imagination (as schematism) and time.

Heidegger emphasizes the significance of the Transcendental Schematism by focusing on the production of an image by imagination. A common understanding of an image is that it is a reproduction of something else, which is why Kant says that the imagination performs a synthesis of reproduction of sensible intuitions. In the Schematism of the Pure Concepts of the Understanding, however, which Kant calls a "synthesis of imagination" (A140/B179), a schema is distinguished from an image. For Kant, "the *image* is a product of the empirical faculty of reproductive imagination," while "the *schema* of sensible concepts . . . is a product and, as it were, a monogram of pure *a priori* imagination" (A142/B181). The schematism is treated under the Transcendental Doctrine of Judgment, which reformulates the question of the Transcendental Deduction: "How, then, is the subsumption of intuitions under pure concepts, the application of a category to appearances, possible?" (A138/B177). The answer is that schemata are *a priori* determinations of time in accordance with rules, which make possible a representation as a determination of time. By accomplishing this time-determination for representations of sensible intuitions, the Schematism of the understanding effects, by means of the transcendental synthesis of imagination, the unity of the manifold of intuition in inner sense. This time-determination of the manifold of sensible intuitions, orders them and allows them to be known by means of categories of the understanding. The schemata, which are products of imagination, "realise . . . the understanding" by allowing its concepts to relate to empirical sensations (A147/B187).

Heidegger affirms that "all conceptual representing is schematism," and brings to Kant's brief section on the Schematism a new attention and significance.[14] Rather than our ordinary understanding of a reproductive image, a schema for Heidegger is a "pure image." This pure image, since it accomplishes the knowledge of objects by means of conceptual understanding in terms of time-determinations, is temporal. "As 'pure image,'" Heidegger writes, "time is the schema-image."[15] He affirms the "inner temporal character of the transcendental power of imagination" because the synthetic production of knowledge which takes place schematically is time-forming. Since "this synthesis is time-forming, the transcendental power of imagination has in itself a pure temporal character."[16] Thus, the transcendental power of imagination, as understood in terms of Kant's Transcendental Schematism, is productive of knowledge in a more primordial way than either sensible intuition or the conceptual understanding. And this production of knowledge is productive insofar as it is temporal, or time-forming. In *The Renewal of the Heidegger–Kant Dialogue*, Frank Schalow claims that Heidegger's engagement with Kantian critical philosophy not only generates a new interpretation of Kant, but also provides the impetus for Heidegger's philosophical breakthrough in *Being and Time*. Schalow suggests that "the chief stimulus for this leap arises from developing the Kantian doctrine of schematism as the key for unmasking a preobjective, prethematic backdrop for comprehending being."[17] Schalow goes on to distinguish Heidegger's later philosophy from Kant by focusing on Heidegger's development of a hermeneutics as mutual implicatory interpretation of being and beings.[18] For the Heidegger of *Being and Time* and *Kant and the Problem of Metaphysics*, however, "because time is central to human cognition, Kant thus effectively shifted the locus of ontology from the nature of things to the nature of time and temporality as the center of the be-ing of man [sic], who experiences things."[19]

Heidegger ontologizes Kantian philosophy as *Dasein's* being-in-the-world. This being-in-the-world is temporal, and the production of temporality for *Dasein* is the work of the transcendental imagination. For Heidegger, the self is determined in and as time; "time as pure self-affection forms the essential structure of subjectivity."[20] Here time is identified with the Kantian "I think," and this means that the ego, rather than being some entity *in* time, in fact *is* time.[21] The Kantian "I think" is the transcendental apperception, which Kant in the Transcendental Deduction introduces as the necessary unity of self-consciousness as it apprehends itself. This transcendental apperception, as a unity which underlies all of our representations, accomplishes the knowledge of objects by means of conceptual categories by uniting sensible intuitions in inner sense as time-determinations.

> This thoroughgoing identity of the apperception of a manifold which is given in intuition contains a synthesis of representations, and is possible only through the consciousness of this synthesis . . . Only in so far, therefore, as I can unite a manifold of given representations in one consciousness, is it possible for me to represent to myself the identity of the consciousness in . . . these representations.
>
> (B133)

It is this unity of apperception which distinguishes human subjectivity or self-consciousness, which Kant avers is "an affair of the understanding alone" (B135), that Heidegger attributes to imagination and identifies with time.

In the next chapter I will examine directly the Transcendental Analytic of the *Critique of Pure Reason* in order to demonstrate the interrelationship of subjectivity, temporality, and imagination. In an important way, all three are defined in terms of each other, which is what Heidegger recognizes with great force and power. Heidegger forges the tools or categories with which to analyze, interrogate, and open up Kantian critical philosophy in terms of schematism and imagination, temporality and subjectivity. In what way, however, does this study of Kant differ from Heidegger's conclusions?

Heidegger recognizes the importance of the transcendental imagination and schematism for an understanding of subjectivity, especially temporal subjectivity. He emphasizes, however, the positive power of imagination for finite transcendence, rather than the negative, disturbing power of imagination for problematizing attempts at knowing. Heidegger argues that time and the Kantian "I think" are the same in the transcendental imagination, and that this production of temporality which is also a production of knowledge is a process or activity which is a finite transcendence. This transcendence is not to be identified with the Kantian transcendent, which lies beyond the realm of sensory appearances and empirical intuitions. Rather, as Schalow writes, it is

> accomplished through imagination, of gathering forth in advance what is to be unified. That is, transcendental apperception unifies all preceding acts of knowledge, because (in conjunction with imagination) it determines in advance all the different combinations of unity... Insofar as it traverses the entire spectrum of possibilities for imparting unity, the "I think" arises from a projective act which culminates in transcendence.[22]

Transcendental imagination is understood as finite transcendence insofar as imagination is understood as the unknown root which underlies and unifies the two stems of sensibility and understanding. John Sallis argues, however, that "a supervenient unity, transcendental imagination as the common root, would violate the very metaphorics of root and stem."[23] This violation occurs because the transcendental imagination as common root is identified by Heidegger with the transcendental apperception, "the self-positing I, of which there is, according to the Kantian text, only thought, not knowledge."[24] If imagination underlies and unifies the two stems of sensibility and understanding, and enables finite transcendence of human knowing, this serves the unity of reason which Kant wants to both defend and critique.[25] Sallis wants to understand imagination in Kant's text not as Heidegger's interpretation implies, "in the sense of a point toward which reason, one of two stems, would be displaced, a new center, as it were, that would somehow resume the role of reason," but as an eccentric rerouting of reason that would, "almost paradoxically, serve to deconstruct both centeredness as such and the metaphorics of root and stem."[26]

Rather than the root of two stems, imagination disrupts the unity and problematizes the joining of sensibility and understanding, even if it is also what allows it to take place. The tentative status of imagination in Kant's First Critique, which sometimes appears as a separate and independent faculty, at other times as a function of the understanding, and at still other times as a somewhat ghostly apparition between the two other faculties, fissures, displaces, and problematizes the deduction of the categories and their application to sensory knowledge at the same time as it makes them possible. The transcendental imagination in its negative sense, then, is not a third faculty which underlies or unifies the other two, but by its occupation of a central position between sensibility and understanding, it functions as a third. This third establishes a triangulation by setting up and mediating a relationship between sensibility and understanding, allowing them to work by pressuring each other but also preventing them from fully functioning in any transcendent way.[27]

The other shortcoming of which Heidegger can be accused in his interpretation of Kant, is his neglect of the *Critique of Judgment*, and the crucial significance of imagination in that text. In the aesthetic judgment of taste, there exists a free play of understanding and imagination, which renders such judgments content-less in any objective sense. Furthermore, in the judgment of the sublime, imagination engages itself in a desperate struggle with reason, in which it attempts to make a presentation of what it intuits in the sublime. The imagination possesses the impressive ability to apprehend to infinity, but it wounds itself in its attempt to present this apprehension to reason. In addition, reason's ability to force the imagination into such a powerful display, which Kant calls a negative pleasure and Deleuze calls a discordant accord, has implications for the configuring of the pure productive imagination which Heidegger achieves in *Kant and the Problem of Metaphysics*. However, Heidegger declares:

> We cannot discuss here the sense in which the pure power of imagination recurs in the *Critique of Judgment* and above all whether it still recurs in express relationship to the laying out of the ground for metaphysics as such which was pointed out earlier.[28]

This parenthetical remark occurs just after Heidegger cites "Kant's dangerous recoil from the abyss opened up by imagination," and occurs "in a way which invites a deconstruction of his own deconstruction of Kant."[29] Even when Heidegger analyzes Kant's doctrine of the beautiful in his *Nietzsche* lectures, he contrasts a beauty devoid of any interest (Kant) with Nietzschean "rapture," thereby avoiding any compromising of beauty's disinterest in the desperate struggle which marks the sublime.[30] Heidegger shrinks back from the abyss of imagination in the sublime judgment of the Third Critique.

II

Jean-François Lyotard, on the other hand, emphasizes the central importance of the *Critique of Judgment* in his interpretation of Kant, and of the significance of the Analytic of the Sublime within the Third Critique. Lyotard develops a general notion of reflective judgment based on Kantian aesthetic judgment rather than Kant's deduction of theoretical judgment of the First Critique. Lyotard thus appends the *Critique of Pure Reason* to the *Critique of Judgment*. That is, for Lyotard, the First Critique is a special (and ultimately unsuccessful) case of the application of reflective judgment or critique understood along the lines of aesthetic judgment. His interpretation of Kantian ideas also propels and to a great extent determines his own project for philosophizing.[31]

I have claimed that Lyotard linguicizes Kant. What does this mean, and how is the *Critique of Judgment* crucial for understanding this phenomenon? In *The Differend: Phrases in Dispute*, Lyotard refers to the "linguistic turn" of Western philosophy, which he associates with Wittgenstein and applies to Kantian texts and ideas.[32] Lyotard appeals to the phrase as the only indubitable object, "because it is immediately presupposed."[33] Phrases can be classified or distributed into different phrase genres, which can loosely be identified with what Kant calls faculties.[34] Many commentators have criticized Kant for his "psychologistic" language of independent faculties or powers of mind which perform independent tasks, as if Kant believed that separate regions of thinking literally exist in the mind, and are specialized into sense intuition, imagination, understanding, and reason.[35] Lyotard helps us to understand the heuristic, provisional, or tentative nature of these faculties, by linguicizing them into phrase genres, or universes of phrase discourses, which can then come into conflict with each other. Division into faculties helps Kant elaborate and wrestle with the heterogeneity of human thinking and reflection, but these divisions should not be reified into self-subsisting entities.

According to Lyotard, phrases exist, as well as different phrase genres, and these different phrase genres, which are incommensurable, come into conflict with each other. This conflict between and among phrases and phrase genres or universes gives rise to what Lyotard calls a differend. In constituting his notion of a differend, Lyotard refers to Kantian Ideas, claiming that an Idea contains no definitive content:

> These situations [Ideas] are not the referents of knowledge phrases. There exist no procedures instituted to establish or refute their reality in the cognitive sense. That is why they give rise to differends.[36]

In the *Critique of Pure Reason*, Kant attempts to establish procedures to secure the objectivity of empirical knowledge. He refers the processes of sensibility and imagination to the understanding. In *Kant's Critical Philosophy*, Gilles Deleuze argues that "only understanding legislates in the faculty of knowledge or in the speculative interest of reason."[37] According to Deleuze, reason functions as a universal tribunal or lawgiver, which delegates authority to the understanding in the First Critique, and rules directly in its own interest in the *Critique of Practical Reason*. In the First Critique we have a hierarchy of faculties, each of which is delegated a certain domain or authority, but all exert their power only under the aegis of reason as a universal tribunal. Lyotard, however, claims that there is no objective, universal tribunal which can judge, evaluate, and arbitrate among conflicting knowledge claims or phrase disputes.

Each heterogeneous phrase engenders a conflict which cannot be resolved cognitively, but can only be felt. Lyotard says that "a phrase that comes along is put into play within a conflict between genres of discourse." This conflict, however, "is a differend, since the success proper to one genre is not the one proper to others."[38] The feeling of the differend which cannot be resolved by a universal tribunal testifies to the heterogeneity or incommensurability of phrase genres. Every Kantian proposition or judgment is referred by Lyotard to a felt differend of phrases. Lyotard calls this differend an abyss which marks "the heterogeneity between ethical phrase and cognitive phrase."[39]

It is important to understand that Lyotard builds his model of the differend among linguistic phrases upon Deleuze's analysis of Kantian faculties. Again, Deleuze separates the faculties and examines their legislative functioning in an accord or discord throughout each of the three critiques. This separation of the faculties is not anthropomorphic, in the sense that we can personify imagination, reason, and understanding as literal protagonists. Lyotard's language of phrases is helpful, however, because it allows an understanding of the complexity and heterogeneity of the processes of human knowing and thinking without reification. Lyotard linguicizes the psychologistic-sounding faculties into linguistic phrase genres. A notion of Kantian faculties as phrase genres in *The Differend* helps to articulate the pragmatic nature of these distinctions already in the Kantian critiques. Finally, Lyotard's conception of a differend will prove instrumental when we turn to his *Lessons on the Analytic of the Sublime*.

Turning more directly to Kant, the order of faculties and mental processes in the functioning of knowledge which Kant sets up in the *Critique of Pure Reason* gets reshuffled and reconstituted in the *Critique of Practical Reason*. The realm of speculative reason is confined to knowledge of things as they appear to us, while practical reason is able to legislate under the moral law of freedom the essence of things as they are in themselves. Theoretical reason is restricted to the sensible world, while moral reason posits a supersensible realm which it can access and actualize. The problem is then the heterogeneity of sensible and supersensible realms, or for Lyotard, the incommensurability of cognitive and moral languages. This problem necessitates the writing of the *Critique of Judgment*.

Kant writes in the introduction to the Third Critique:

Hence an immense gulf is fixed between the domain of the concept of nature, the sensible, and the domain of the concept of freedom, the supersensible, so that no transition from the sensible to the supersensible . . . is possible.[40]

Kant writes the *Critique of Judgment* in order to provide a bridge between speculative and practical philosophy. In the course of writing the Third Critique, however, Kant develops an alternate notion of reflective judgment to the one he lays out in the First Critique. Lyotard argues in *Lessons on the Analytic of the Sublime* that this model of aesthetic judgment is more appropriate and more accurate than the model of theoretical judgment which functions in terms of a deduction of categories and subsumption of sense impressions under objective categories, which Kant develops in the *Critique of Pure Reason*. Lyotard claims that "if the third Critique fulfills its mission of unifying the field of philosophy, it does so . . . by making manifest, in the name of the aesthetic, the reflexive manner of thinking that is at work in the critical text as a whole."[41] Put simply, "feelings orientate a critique," and it is the feeling of teleological finality which Kant hopes can provide a bridge from moral freedom to nature in which nature can be attributed a purpose in analogy with human freedom or purposefulness. Lyotard also claims that feelings orient a critique at a more basic level, because all sensations or intuitions in their immediacy demand a representation which calls for reflection and critique as soon as a person becomes aware of her intuitions as aesthetic intuitions.

Lyotard claims that aesthetic or reflective judgment has two components: it is heuristic and tautegorical. Lyotard uses tautegorical to mean subjective, that is, our judgments are self-referential and do not necessarily contain any objective content.[42] Heuristic refers to the possibility of referring our intuitions and judgments to anything else, especially another thinking human being.[43] In the *Critique of Judgment*, Kant claims that a judgment of taste is "a judgment whose determining basis cannot be other than subjective."[44] Because aesthetic judgment consists in a free play of imagination and understanding, the independent status of imagination compromises the objectivity of such judgments, and prevents one from subsuming aesthetic intuitions under categories of the understanding. So an aesthetic judgment of taste lacks objective content, and this is what Lyotard refers to when he calls reflective judgment tautegorical. The other element of a judgment of taste for Kant is that it makes a claim to subjective universality, that is, "if someone likes something and is conscious that he himself [sic] does so without interest, then he cannot help judging that it must contain a basis for being liked [that holds] for everyone."[45] The subjective universality, which Kant defines as the presumption that an aesthetic judgment could be held in the same way by any rational being, is what Lyotard refers to by the term heuristic.

Lyotard opposes the objective knowledge (even if only in the realm of appearances) of the *Critique of Pure Reason*, to the reflective knowledge of the *Critique of Judgment*. This reflective knowledge becomes the basis for a general understanding of thinking and judging, for Lyotard, rather than merely a special case, as it is in Kant. Reflective judgment, because it is aesthetic, is oriented and animated by feeling, and it gives rise to conflicts between and among faculties or phrase genres which constitute differends that cannot be resolved. Such differends cannot be resolved because one cannot appeal to a higher cognitive authority to mediate or arbitrate disputes. Despite Kant's intentions, Lyotard levels the hierarchical status of the faculties, echoing Deleuze for whom the *Critique of Judgment* represents "a disorder of all the senses."[46]

Why does the Third Critique represent a "disorder of all the senses?" Lyotard puts his finger on the heart of the disorder when he focuses on the category of the sublime. The special case of the sublime judgment provides Lyotard with his notion of the differend. Deleuze describes the three Critiques as different relations or organizations of the faculties, for which in each Critique he asks, which faculty legislates? Deleuze distinguishes two definitions of faculty: he treats four faculties of mind as a specific source of representation—sensation, imagination, understanding, and reason—and details their interaction in what he calls the higher faculties (what representations can be related to) of knowledge (First Critique), desire (Second Critique), and faculty of the feeling of pleasure and pain (Third Critique). In the aesthetic judgment of taste, understanding and imagination work in harmony and free play, while in the First Critique sensation and imagination work in the service of the understanding, and in the *Critique of Practical Reason* reason legislates in its own interest.[47] For Lyotard, the sublime represents the case where a differend occurs between reason and imagination.[48] According to Kant, reason is the faculty which legislates overall, and functions as the highest tribunal for the faculties of mind. In its differend with imagination in the sublime, however, reason is also an interested party. Lyotard disallows the role of reason to play both judge and litigant, arguing that if reason allows itself to be a part of the dispute, then it cannot appeal to itself as a higher authority to press its claim. Since no higher faculty than reason exists, Lyotard concludes that no faculty exists which can resolve a differend among or between the individual faculties. In *The Differend*, Lyotard uses the victims of the Nazi Holocaust as a test case for his theory. The victims of Auschwitz cannot participate in a court of law, and prosecute a case against their torturers, insofar as their status as litigants deprives them of their victimhood, by submitting their experience to a universal tribunal for judgment. This brutal wronging of Holocaust victims cannot be universally established, according to Lyotard, only felt in a silence which is deafening because it shatters rational thought.

Influenced more in its particulars by Hannah Arendt than by Kant, Lyotard's court case is loosely based on the trial of Adolf Eichmann.[49]

The differend between imagination and reason in the sublime judgment extends for Lyotard to every possible judgment, because it infects the process of subjective judging itself. Judgment is subjective because it is based on a model of reflective judgment which constitutes Kant's aesthetic judgment, according to Lyotard. Furthermore, an aesthetic judgment of taste cannot be cordoned off from an aesthetic judgment of the sublime. "Sublime feeling can be thought of as an extreme case of the beautiful," because the feeling of the sublime is merely the tendency of the imagination to go wild in its proliferation of forms.[50] The sublime asserts itself when the imagination is prompted, by the mind's contemplation of an object, to strive "to progress toward infinity."[51] Lyotard writes that the "aesthetic comprehension of the whole (at one time) of a very large or infinite series is what reason demands of the imagination and what provokes the sublime emotion."[52] This power to progress to infinity of imagination outstrips the ability of understanding to comprehend conceptually, whereupon reason enters the scene and demands the presentation of this apprehension of infinity, or "absolute totality as a real idea," which imagination is unable to do.[53]

The feeling of the sublime is thus a negative pleasure. It is negative, because the imagination wounds itself in its unsuccessful attempt to present its apprehension of the infinite to reason. However it is also a pleasure because reason is powerful enough to rein in imagination, as it were, and bring about a harmony of the senses amid such disharmony.[54] Lyotard claims that

> the imagination does violence to itself in order to present a magnitude, which is a sign of the subjective absolute of magnitude (magnitude itself). Moreover, the imagination does violence to itself because reason has the strength to demand this of it.[55]

Kant says that "sublime is what even to be able to think proves that the mind has a power surpassing any standard of sense."[56] The displeasure involves the inability to distinctly conceive or conceptualize the sublime, because even though we can "think" the sublime, we cannot present the unpresentable. The pleasure involves the *power* of the mind to acknowledge its own ability to strive toward the infinite as well as its power to rein itself in.

With his notion of the differend, Lyotard challenges the primacy of reason as a tribunal to adjudicate disputes, as well as its ability to contain the disturbing power of imagination in the sublime in a harmony of the faculties. He suggests that the sublime evokes a feeling which cannot be conceived, only felt by means of "an insensible passability" which he calls an *an-aisthesis* or "anesthetics" in *Heidegger and "the jews"*.[57] Lyotard appends the *Critique of Pure Reason* to the *Critique of Judgment*, making the Third Critique the theoretical model for his philosophizing. He does not demonstrate, however, the implications of his reading of the sublime for the First Critique, nor does he develop the consequences of the disappearance of the understanding in the sublime, both of which are interconnected. Lyotard does provide a different reading of Kantian aesthetics, reflection, and judgment, which, while not specifically indebted to Heidegger, can still be evaluated as in the spirit of *Kant and the Problem of Metaphysics*.

Conclusion

Heidegger provides important and insightful tools to read and interpret the *Critique of Pure Reason*. He brings together imagination, subjectivity and temporality in the Transcendental Deduction and the Schematism in a way which emphasizes the fusion of all three in a positive knowing which is characterized as a finite transcendence. Heidegger stresses the positive power of the productive imagination, but he neglects what I am calling the negative imagination and its crucial significance in the *Critique of Judgment*. Lyotard builds upon Deleuze to provide a reading of Kant in which the Third Critique is central, and his interpretation of the sublime allows a reexamination of the status of objective knowledge in the First Critique.

Both Heidegger and Lyotard develop novel interpretations of Kant which provide important resources for their own philosophies. Heidegger's reading of the *Critique of Pure Reason* in *Kant and the Problem of Metaphysics* is central to his constructive philosophy in *Being and Time*, and it also provides the resources for Heidegger to move beyond this interpretation in his later philosophy. Lyotard's reading of the *Critique of Judgment* provides the impetus for his constructive philosophical work in *The Differend*, even though *Lessons on the Analytic of the Sublime* is written afterwards. By reading together Heidegger (First Critique) and Lyotard (Third Critique), one can develop a project for reading the *Critique of Judgment*, along Lyotardian lines, back into the *Critique of Pure Reason*, illuminated by Heidegger's insights, in a way which is highly significant for philosophical and theological thinking. The sublime will prove not to be contained within the confines of the *Critique of Judgment*, but will be shown to affect and infect the *Critique of Pure Reason* via the transcendental imagination, or a reading of the Schematism of the Pure Concepts of the Understanding. I will return to the *Critique of Judgment* in Chapter Five, but first the interconnections of temporality, subjectivity, and imagination in the first half of the *Critique of Pure Reason* need to be explicated and interrogated.

4 Temporality, subjectivity and imagination

Kant *avec* Deleuze

Introduction

Chapters Four through Six develop an original reading of Kant pressured by the insights of Deleuze and Derrida, with the interpretations of Heidegger and Lyotard in the background. In this chapter I present Kant's interpretation of time, self and imagination in the first part of the *Critique of Pure Reason*. The Kantian conceptions of time, self, and imagination are intended to assist the work of the understanding in order to secure the objectivity of empirical knowledge, even though such determinate knowledge is restricted to the phenomenal realm of appearances. In *Kant's Critical Philosophy*, however, and also in *Difference and Repetition*, Deleuze troubles this interpretation by showing how Kant's combination of temporality and subjectivity fissures the status of knowledge and the knowing subject within the realm of appearances. Chapter Five returns to the *Critique of Judgment*, and analyzes the relationship of imagination and understanding in the feelings of beauty and the sublime.[1] This transformed awareness of the disturbing power of the imagination, along with the implicit impotence of the understanding, is then related back to the First Critique, where it has striking consequences. The breakdown or disappearance of the understanding in the *Critique of Judgment* compromises its objective or determinative status in the *Critique of Pure Reason*. Finally, all of these themes converge in Kant's brief chapter on "the schematism of the pure concepts of the understanding," which is the subject of Chapter Six, where an analogy will be made between Kant's transcendental imagination and Derrida's notion of *différance*.

I

Kant restricts objective human knowledge to the realm of things as they appear to us empirically, and disallows any knowledge of things as they are in themselves. This transcendental idealism is not a solipsistic idealism, and in fact Kant is constrained to make a "refutation of idealism" in the second edition of the First Critique (B274–9). Rather, transcendental idealism is the only way Kant can secure the objectivity of empirical phenomena, or what he calls empirical realism (A371).[2] Any attempt to understand things as they are in themselves metaphysically leads either to dogmatism or to skepticism (B23). In order to secure objective knowledge of empirical phenomena, Kant is forced to posit a gap between things as they appear and (those same) things as they are in themselves. This problem drives the *Critique of Pure Reason*, which is written in order to overcome a seeming conflict or antinomy of reason with itself, and which can only be solved by differentiating the world as it appears to human sensibility and the world as it is in itself, apart from any human understanding. In a letter to Christian Garve dated 21 September 1789, Kant remarks:

> It was not from the investigation of the existence of God, of immortality, and so on, that I started but from the antinomy of pure reason, "The world has a beginning—; it has no beginning—," and so on . . . These were what first awoke me from my dogmatic slumbers and drove me to the critique of reason itself in order to end the scandal of reason's ostensible contradictions with itself.[3]

One of the questions this study raises is whether Kant has ended the scandal and secured the empirical realm of phenomena for objective validity, or whether there still exists a gap at the heart of the realm of appearances, at the center of the *Critique of Pure Reason*.

Kant begins the First Critique with the Transcendental Aesthetic, and he introduces space and time as the (only) two pure concepts of sensible intuition. That is, temporality and spatiality constitute the *a priori* formal conditions of possibility for any sensible intuition whatsoever. Time and space are each essentially one, such that every particular intuition within a certain time and space is merely a delimitation of one infinite temporality or spatiality. "Space is essentially one;" it is "represented as an infinite given magnitude" (A25/B39). Time, likewise, "has only one dimension," and "every determinate magnitude of time is possible only through limitations of one single time that underlies it" (A31–2/B47–8).

Time and space occupy a privileged and unique role in Kant's philosophy. These concepts are the only concepts of the intuition, whereas the understanding has many concepts which belong to a table of categories. Furthermore, the concepts of time and space are so basic and self-evident to Kant that he subjects them to a transcendental deduction at once in the Transcendental Aesthetic, by tracing them back to their sources as the condition of possibility of geometry (space) and human perception (time). Space and time are the two *a priori* forms of sensory intuitions. Why, then, does Heidegger privilege time and temporality, and why does this study focus primarily on time rather than space in its connection with subjectivity and judgment? Kant distinguishes time and space by referring space to outer sense, while time is "the form of inner sense" (A33/B49).

Space refers to the representation of objects as external to us, while time has to do with our inner states of mind, that is, how we represent ourselves to ourselves. Because of this split, and also due to Kant's emphasis on apperception or subjectivity, Kant declares that "time is the formal *a priori* condition of all appearances whatsoever" (A34/B50). Space as the pure form of outer intuition, is limited to the *a priori* condition of outer appearances alone. Kant disqualifies space from the inner sanctum of human knowing. Time, on the other hand, is "the immediate condition of inner appearances . . . and thereby the mediate condition of outer appearances" (A34/B50–1).

In this way, Kant presents space as secondary and derivative, not because objects do not really exist "out there," but because time is more fundamental to subjective human experience and knowing. Ultimately, therefore, "all appearances whatsoever, that is, all objects of the senses, are in time, and necessarily stand in time-relations" (A34/B51). This theory of time-determination, which applies to all appearances and perceptions, extends throughout the *Critique of Pure Reason*. In order for a person to have an empirical or phenomenal experience, it must take place in time as a mode of temporal awareness. That is, it must be temporally distinguished or successive in order to be recognizable as an experience. Such a conception underlies the insights developed in the Analogies of Experience, which are simply "three modes of time:" duration, succession, and coexistence (A177/B219). Kant states in the first edition at the outset of the Analogies that "all appearances are, as regards their existence, subject *a priori* to rules determining their relation to one another in time" (A177). This sentence echoes the one above from the Transcendental Aesthetic.

For the first analogy, the "principle of permanence of substance," Kant explains that "apprehension of the manifold of appearance is always successive, and is therefore always changing" (A182/B225). In order to experience an intuition as successive, however, one must have an *a priori* notion of substance as substrate, within which change can occur and to which change can relate.

> We require an underlying ground which exists *at all times*, that is, something *abiding* and *permanent*, of which all change and coexistence are only so many ways (modes of time) in which the permanent exists.
>
> (A182/B226)

We do not experience the unity of time as it is in itself (which is not a quality possessed by objects in themselves), but we must posit time as an infinite unity in order to explain the specific appearances which take place successively within time. In this way, according to the first analogy of experience, time is the substratum of all appearances. Note that the Schematism, which will be discussed later, or "the schema of the concepts of the understanding," is also defined in terms of a "transcendental determination of time" (A139/B178).

Of course, accepting Kant's accounts of necessity or substance defined in terms of duration, and causality understood as succession, one could still ask questions about the nature of coexistence, community, or reciprocity.[4] Since "coexistence is the existence of the manifold in one and the same time," how could different phenomena be differentiated which occur at the same time, except spatially? Kant must have been aware of this problem, because in the second edition he replaces the time-specific definition of the Analogies with a more general definition. He writes at the start of the third analogy that "all substances, in so far as they can be perceived to coexist in *space*, are in thoroughgoing reciprocity" (B256, emphasis mine). This alteration mitigates the duality of time and space in the Transcendental Aesthetic (although the relation of time and space is not restated there in the B edition), and suggests that temporality and spatiality understood as differentiation in human perception are perhaps more equivalent.

Time is petitioned as a fundamental *a priori*, which cannot be represented as such, but must accompany or be invoked by any possible representation. The inability to simply represent time in itself leads Kant to admit that "we cannot obtain for ourselves a representation of time, which is not an object of outer intuition, except under the image of a line, which we draw" (B156). In other words, we cannot represent time to ourselves internally, as it exists in inner sense, but only externally, that is, spatially. This inability to represent time conceptually except in terms of space, specifically a line, is the fundamental insight underlying Henri Bergson's critical notion of duration, which is a dynamic and temporal notion that cannot be spatialized.[5] My concern in any case is not with space and time as such, but the crucial importance that the concept of temporality plays within the framework of Kant's Critique.

II

Temporality is emphasized and privileged in the First Critique because of its essential connection (for Kant) with subjectivity. As transcendental unity of apperception, subjectivity becomes crucial in Kant's Transcendental Deduction of the Pure Concepts of the Understanding. Kant uses the term deduction to mean a juridical justification for how the human mind combines the manifold of sensory intuitions with the categories, or the pure concepts of the understanding, which provide unity and objective knowledge.[6] The combination of the manifold is "an act of spontaneity of the faculty of representation" which "must be entitled understanding" (B130).[7] Kant calls this act of understanding, which combines intuition and concept, synthesis. The possibility of synthesis depends for Kant on the existence of a transcendental unity of apperception, which means that in order for representations of an object to be unified under a concept, they must refer to some at least posited unity to which they can relate in the subject. Subjectivity, here termed the transcendental unity of apperception, functions as a substratum for the connectability of successive representations in the same way that temporality does in the first analogy of substance. Kant argues that "it must be possible for the 'I think' to accompany all my representation; for otherwise something would be represented in me which could not be thought at all" (B131–2).

Pure apperception, as the formal unity which must accompany all representations, is distinguished from empirical apperception, which is simply the perception of self as an object of experience or appearance (B132). A.C. Ewing writes:

> The transcendental unity of apperception is to be sharply distinguished from any object of ordinary empirical perception . . . Yet in Kant's view it is equally erroneous to hypostasize it into a pure Ego theory of the self according to which we are aware of an "I" over and above all our experiences and the complex unity they form.[8]

As a bare unity of experience, the transcendental apperception is also distinguished from the noumenal self or soul, which cannot be speculatively known but must be practically thought in order to provide a basis for moral law. The identification of the transcendental unity of apperception with the noumenal self as it is in itself gives rise later in the First Critique to the Paralogisms of Pure Reason.

A paralogism is a contradiction that occurs when reason reifies the self as a thing-in-itself without attending to the process of subjectivity which constitutes the I as an empirical entity. Kant is specifically concerned with the hypostatization of personal immortality, which cannot be proved, only assumed as a practical postulate of moral reason. P.F. Strawson argues that to confuse the reality of the noumenal self or soul as an object of possible experience (which is not possible) with the transcendental unity of apperception or consciousness needed to secure empirical knowledge "confuses the unity of experiences with the experience of unity."[9] The transcendental unity of apperception is a transcendental unity of self-consciousness, which must be assumed in a formal, analytic sense in order to be able to think anything at all. "Only in so far, therefore, as I can unite a manifold of given representations in one consciousness," Kant writes, "is it possible for me to represent to myself the identity of the consciousness in [i.e., throughout] these representations" (B133). Kant empties the Cartesian *cogito* of any empirical content, but retains it as an empty, formal, and bare unity for the connection of intuitions with concepts by means of the activity of the understanding. Kant calls the principle of apperception "the highest principle in the whole sphere of human knowledge" (B135).

Since it serves to connect particular sense intuitions to universal and objectively valid conceptual categories, the unity of apperception guarantees the objective validity of knowledge. This objective validity is restricted to knowledge of phenomena, to be sure, but it is only "through this unity of consciousness that an object . . . [as appearance] is first known" (B138). Kant concludes: "The synthetic unity of consciousness is, therefore, an objective condition of all knowledge" (B138). So objectivity (restricted to appearances) relies ultimately on identity of subjectivity, and this is the conclusion of both Dieter Henrich and Paul Guyer.

Henrich distinguishes between two themes of the Transcendental Deduction understood as claims: does the validity of the deduction rest on a principle of objectivity or identity? Henrich comes down on the side of identity, or subjectivity.[10] This identity is not subjectively psychological, however, and Henrich claims that the second edition of the First Critique represents an advance on the first edition because here Kant "established that intuitions are subject to the categories insofar as they, as intuitions, already possess unity," that is, unity of apperception. This transcendental unity of apperception is ambiguously subjective in the first edition, according to Henrich, but in the second edition the transcendental unity of apperception is clearer and more functionally integral to the Transcendental Deduction. Henrich concludes that Kant based his entire system on "the unifying principle of the unity of self-consciousness."[11]

Guyer introduces two further distinctions, dividing identity and objectivity into strong and weak forms, and he argues that only a weak argument from identity works for Kant. This argument from identity which Guyer supports is not characteristic of the Transcendental Deduction, however, which exhibits a very strong form of identity argument, based on the transcendental unity of apperception. Rather, Guyer locates Kant's "successful" weak identity argument in the Schematism and in the Analogies, with their explicit conceptions of identity as time-determination:

> Kant's original conception of a transcendental theory of experience, on which the task for a transcendental deduction was identified by an abstract discussion of synthetic *a priori* judgments but was solved only by the theory of time-determination implied by the "analogies of

experience," resurfaces in the course of the "Schematism" and "System of All Principles of Pure Understanding".[12]

The Transcendental Deduction is unique in that Kant does not explicitly connect the deduction of the categories to temporality or time-determination, as he does in the Transcendental Aesthetic, the Schematism, and also in the Analogies of Experience. He does, however, explain that the synthesis of understanding is an act, which implies that it takes place temporally, and he discusses apperception or subjectivity in the deduction in an analogous way to temporality in the Analogies. As Guyer argues, and as I will demonstrate in Chapter Five, subjectivity and temporality are joined even more explicitly in the Schematism.[13]

The one place Kant does discuss time in the Transcendental Deduction is in the sentence already quoted about representations of time being impossible to obtain except in spatial terms. There he connects an experience of oneself in time to an intuition of oneself as an object of inner sense. Kant makes essentially the same argument about subjectivity as he did about temporality.

> We must also recognize, as regards inner sense, that by means of it we intuit ourselves only as we are inwardly affected by ourselves; in other words, that, so far as inner intuition is concerned, we know our own subject as appearance, not as it is in itself.
>
> (B156)

Subjectivity or temporality cannot be known as they are in themselves; all that can be known are the empirical appearances which occur within time. One can experience oneself as an object of experience, but Kant distinguishes this from the transcendental unity of apperception. The transcendental unity of apperception is a formal unity which underlies and unifies particular experiences or intuitions of the manifold. Temporality as the form of inner sense, not an object of inner sense, is one, unlimited dimension. Experience depends on the unity of apperception to provide connection and identity, that is, to be thought as a representation. Experience is also a determination or mode of time, which allows an object to exist and be known as such.

Kant assigns time to the *a priori* form of sensible intuitions, while he reserves subjectivity or apperception for the conceptual activity of the understanding, but they both perform the same function.[14] Heidegger draws the conclusion: "time and the 'I think' ... they are the same."[15] Why? Because the unity of apperception or self-consciousness ensures the deduction of the concepts of the understanding, and it is the transcendental imagination which performs the activity or procedure of relating the sensory intuitions to the categories of the understanding, that is, makes thinking and knowledge possible.

The Transcendental Deduction works out this procedure, and the ultimate result of this process is an understanding of what Kant calls transcendental judgment. Judgment "will be the faculty of subsuming under rules" (A132/B171), but Kant also claims that "judgment is a peculiar talent which can be practised only, and cannot be taught" (A133/B172). Furthermore, the Schematism of the Pure Concepts of the Understanding, which is carried out by the name of the transcendental imagination, occurs under the heading of Transcendental Doctrine of Judgment. Finally, the schema is a transcendental determination of time.

III

How is the imagination related to these interconnected notions of subjectivity and temporality? To discover how imagination functions in the Transcendental Deduction, I will again take a cue from Heidegger and examine the difference between the first and second editions of the First Critique. In the second edition of the *Critique of Pure Reason*, published in 1787, Kant completely rewrites the section on the Transcendental Deduction of the Categories. In the section on the Analytic of Concepts, which remains identical in both editions, Kant claims, as noted in Chapter Two, that "synthesis in general . . . is the mere result of the power of imagination, a blind but indispensable function of the soul" (A78/B103). "To bring this synthesis to concepts," however, "is a function which belongs to the understanding" (A78/B103). This statement reflects Kant's distinction between imagination and understanding that informs both editions of the First Critique.

Heidegger focuses on the mediating position of the imagination between sensory intuitions and concepts of the understanding, and argues that Kant understates the importance of imagination in bringing thoughts to representation. Kant slights the role of imagination because he fears that its significance compromises the objectivity of phenomenal understanding. Against Heidegger, it must be insisted that in both editions the transcendental imagination plays an important role. The transcendental imagination, as will be shown, also plays a crucial part in the Schematism, which is identical in both editions. In each edition, however, the function of the transcendental power of imagination is ultimately granted to the understanding.

In the A edition, after establishing the transcendental unity of apperception as a condition for relating the categories to intuitions, Kant claims that "the transcendental unity of apperception thus relates to the pure synthesis of imagination, as an *a priori* condition of the possibility of all combination of the manifold in one knowledge" (A118). Kant distinguishes between the pure productive imagination (*Einbildungskraft*), which alone is transcendental and *a priori*, and the reproductive imagination, which "rests upon empirical conditions" (A118). The productive imagination is what makes reproduction possible, while the reproductive imagination merely reproduces empirical intuitions. Therefore, "the transcendental unity of the synthesis of imagination is the pure form of all possible knowledge" (A118).

This statement sounds impressive, but Kant never meant to assign the importance of the transcendental unity of the synthesis of imagination directly to the faculty of imagination. Kant states, in the A Deduction of the First Critique:

> The unity of apperception in relation to the synthesis of imagination is the understanding; and this same unity, with reference to the transcendental synthesis of the imagination, the pure understanding.
>
> (A119)

Heidegger is correct to charge Kant with shrinking back from the disturbing power of the imagination, but even in the first edition, according to this reading, Kant has already shrunk back. On the other hand, in both editions, Kant recognizes and reveals the importance for knowing of the transcendental synthesis of imagination. In *Constituting Critique: Kant's Writing as Critical Praxis*, Willi Goetschel argues that the Transcendental Deduction

> forms a labyrinth of the concept of the "I," out of which only the self-spun thread of the synthetic unity of apperception is able to guide us. The synthesis that is its prerequisite, however, is a product of the imagination . . . On this point, the second version of the deduction basically alters nothing. It only situates imagination deeper, systematically, and removes its dominant character, by simultaneously anchoring it that much more definitely in the concept of synthesis.[16]

As I noted above, however, Dieter Henrich argues that the second edition more successfully emphasizes and demonstrates the integral importance of the transcendental unity of apperception, although Henrich does not focus on the status of imagination in the respective editions.

Kant merely wants to assign the power or ability of this phenomenal knowing to the understanding, in order to safeguard its objectivity, at least in the realm of appearances. In the second edition, Kant is explicit: "the transcendental synthesis of imagination . . . is an action of the understanding on the sensibility" (B152). What, then, is the difference between the A and the B Deduction with regard to the imagination? My argument is that Kant grants independence to the imagination in the first edition, in a way that threatens its dependence on the understanding. The independence of imagination rests upon its identification with a distinct synthesis. Kant claims, in the A Deduction, that "knowledge is (essentially) a whole in which representations stand compared and connected" (A97). This activity of knowing Kant calls a spontaneity: "receptivity can make knowledge possible only when combined with spontaneity" (A97). The activity of spontaneity which produces knowledge Kant calls synthesis, and he distinguishes three syntheses which are found in all knowledge, "namely, the apprehension of representations as modifications of the mind in intuition, their reproduction in imagination, and their recognition in a concept" (A97). Heidegger treats all three syntheses as modes of time which apply to pure synthesis, or imagination, in general. He concludes that as a result of all three syntheses, pure apprehension as pure self-apprehension, pure reproduction as pure self-reproduction, and finally pure recognition as pure self-recognition, "time as pure self-affection forms the essential structure of subjectivity."[17]

In the first edition, Kant treats the imagination separately as a distinct synthesis, which makes possible the "reproducibility of all appearances" (A133). This synthesis of imagination occupies a middle position between a synthesis of apprehension and one of recognition (keep in mind, also, that imagination is the power which enables synthesis in general). This threefold synthesis gives the impression that each synthesis corresponds with a particular faculty or power of mind which carries out this synthesis. The synthesis of apprehension relates to intuition, the synthesis of reproduction to imagination, while the synthesis of recognition in a concept refers to the transcendental unity of apperception or "formal unity of consciousness" which is a procedure of conceptual understanding.

This conclusion creates a problem, however, because of the spontaneity of synthesis, which seems to preclude its application to intuition, which is a passive faculty (as opposed to imagination, understanding, and reason, which are all active). What power performs the synthesis of apprehension in intuition? It will later become clear that it is imagination which is responsible for the synthesis of apprehension, and Kant in the second edition reduces the synthesis of reproduction to apprehension. In the B Deduction Kant collapses the three syntheses into two, and assigns the imagination to the figural synthesis, while the intellectual synthesis "is carried out by the understanding alone, without the aid of the imagination" (B152). Imagination, "owing to the subjective condition under which alone it can give to the concepts of the understanding a corresponding intuition, belongs to sensibility" (B151). The figurative synthesis, which is the work of imagination, and in its productive power transcendental imagination, replaces and collapses the twofold synthesis of apprehension and reproduction of the first edition. The intellectual synthesis is the work of the understanding alone, and relates to the synthesis of recognition in a concept based on the unity of transcendental apperception, which alone gives objective validity to the categories. Kant claims that the figural synthesis, which he calls the transcendental synthesis of imagination, must be distinguished from the purely intellectual synthetic combination of transcendental unity of apperception. Imagination, Kant holds, despite its exclusion from intellectual-conceptual synthesis, is that faculty which can represent an object without its being present in intuition. This function of imagination will become crucial for understanding the workings of the Schematism.

If synthesis is the "mere result of the power of imagination," and if, as I have tried to establish, the synthetic character of our knowing for Kant lies in time-determination based on unity of apperception, then imagination, temporality, and subjectivity coalesce in the First Critique, despite Kant's efforts at times to keep them apart. Specifically, Kant needs to separate the work of imagination from that of understanding, which is a function of bringing synthesis to concepts by means of the unity of transcendental apperception, in order to insure the objective validity of the Deduction of the categories of the understanding and their application to sensory intuitions. Kant wrestles with the central importance of imagination, especially the transcendental or pure productive imagination, which mediates all of our knowledge, but he attempts to eliminate any independence from sensory intuition and any confusion of its role and power with that of the understanding. In fact, Kant further subordinates imagination to understanding, even in the figural synthesis, when he distinguishes inner sense from apperception. Kant argues that inner sense "represents to consciousness even our own selves only as we appear to ourselves, not as we are in ourselves. For we intuit ourselves only as we are inwardly *affected*" (B153). This affect of intuition is what Kant calls inner sense, and he claims that this is the result of "the transcendental act of imagination (synthetic influence of the understanding upon inner sense), which I have entitled figurative synthesis" (B154). This act performed by the understanding "under the title of a *transcendental synthesis of imagination*," makes up inner sense and is performed or enacted upon the passive subject (B153). This is to be clearly distinguished from apperception, which, "as the source of all *combination*, applies to the manifold of *intuitions in general*, and in the guise of the *categories*, prior to all sensible intuition, to *objects in general*" (B154).

Despite Kant's efforts to separate transcendental imagination and transcendental apperception, however, the question may be raised whether they are essentially the same process or procedure. Heidegger answers this question with an emphatic yes. He demonstrates how time, subjectivity and imagination come together in the *Critique of Pure Reason*, even though Kant wants to prevent this unity. The positive power of imagination allows for knowing, and "time as such [as transcendental synthesis or imagination] has the character of selfhood."[18]

IV

According to Deleuze, however, the introduction of time into the interiority of the subject splits the self, and makes impossible its unification by means of imagination. In the Preface to *Kant's Critical Philosophy*, Deleuze elaborates four poetic formulas which represent the impact of Kantian philosophy. The first two deal with time and the self, respectively, but they are also intrinsically connected. Quoting Hamlet's statement, "the time is out of joint," Deleuze claims that Kant reverses the relationship between time and movement. Prior to Kant, time was subordinated to movement, or "the cardinal points through which the periodical movements that it measures pass."[19] That is, time is determined by the interval or number which measures its passage. With the *Critique of Pure Reason*, however, movement is subordinated to time, because movement or succession can only take place within our representation of time, which is not time itself. "Time is no longer defined by succession," Deleuze writes, "because succession concerns only things and movements which are in time."[20]

Succession, simultaneity, and permanence are modes or determinations of time, but time itself does not change. "Appearances may, one and all, vanish; but time (as the universal condition of their possibility) cannot itself be removed" (A31/B46). Time is "the form of everything that changes and moves, but it is an immutable Form which does not change."[21]

The second of Deleuze's poetic formulas is taken from Rimbaud, but applied to Kant: "I is another." Kant splits the Ego which exists in time as an object of empirical experience, which undergoes succession and change, from the I which "is an act which constantly carries out a synthesis of time."[22] Time brings about this splitting of the self, because it divides the empirical self which is experienced within time from the transcendental unity of apperception which performs the temporal synthesis which defines knowing. "Thus time moves into the subject" which, as the form of inner sense, makes knowledge possible only at the cost of splitting the active, knowing subject from the passive self which is known as an object, appearance, or representation. Deleuze concludes that "our interiority constantly divides us from ourselves, splits us in two: a splitting in two which never runs its course, since time has no end."[23]

What are the consequences of this fracturing or fissuring of the I? In order to secure the objectivity of phenomenal appearance, Kant must deny knowledge of the supersensible, or objects as they are in themselves (the *Ding an sich*). The transcendental self or ego, as Kant explains in the second part of the First Critique, is a regulative idea of which we lack empirical experience, along with the ideas of world and of God. We do not have theoretical knowledge of these ideas, but we can have access to them in practical reason via the moral law. Kant creates a split or a gap between the phenomenal and the noumenal realm, one of which can be empirically known, the other of which must be practically posited. This split between the world we experience and the world as it is in itself is immensely troubling for philosophical understanding, and Kant's followers immediately tried to overcome it by means of speculative idealism.[24]

The problem Deleuze raises, however, is that of a split or gap *within* the realm of phenomenal appearances. One can identify three distinct selves in Kant. The first is the noumenal self which is a thing in itself, which for Kant guarantees the moral realm or practical knowledge. The second is the empirical or phenomenal self which is experienced as an object of representation within time. The third distinct Kantian self is the transcendental unity of apperception, or the active self which performs the syntheses of time-determinations. If this last self is identified with the noumenal self, then not only do we commit a paralogism of pure reason, according to Kant, but we cannot have the theoretical knowledge of it upon which it is necessary to base a deduction of objective knowledge of appearances. If it is a distinct third self, however, then it fractures the unity of empirical appearances Kant has worked so hard to secure. Heidegger identifies the third self with imagination, and suggests that it represents a unitary primordial subjectivity which underlies the other two selves. Deleuze, however, emphasizes the disruptive capacity of what could only be a negative imagination, because it upsets the fragile stability of Kant's alleged duality. Deleuze does not explicitly discuss the role of imagination in the *Critique of Pure Reason*, but he affirms the fractured status of the I and claims that this status has to do with time. In *Difference and Repetition*, Deleuze states that "it is as though the *I* were fractured from one end to the other: fractured by the pure and empty form of time." Deleuze claims that this fracturing of the I also brings about the death of God, or at least a Western (Cartesian) God which "survives as long as the I enjoys a subsistence, a simplicity and an identity which express the entirety of its resemblance to the divine."[25] He continues: "If the greatest initiative of transcendental philosophy was to introduce the form of time into thought as such, then this pure and empty form in turn signifies indissolubly the death of God, the fractured I and the passive self."[26]

In a similar way, Dieter Henrich claims that an implication of "the fundamental argument of the whole Critique" is that "our consciousness has the peculiarity of being 'empty,'" because it is "always a making-conscious whose necessary inner unity causes us to give it the name 'I'."[27] This emptiness is the result of what Deleuze calls the fracturing of the unity of self-consciousness by time, as the condition for the possibility of unifying empirical experience.

In *Kant's Critical Philosophy*, Gilles Deleuze points out the two distinct senses of the word "faculty" in Kant. Faculty can mean those faculties or capacities of the mind which contribute to thinking, or sources of representation, such as imagination, reason, understanding, and intuition. Deleuze also understands faculties to mean those areas which are represented by the relationships among faculties of mind: knowledge, desire, and feeling.[28] The latter three correspond to the three Kantian critiques. For Deleuze, the relationship among these faculties in each of the three critiques is significant, and we have seen the importance of Deleuze's analysis for Lyotard in Chapter Three. In the *Critique of Pure Reason*, the understanding legislates in place of reason in the interests of phenomenal knowledge. In the Second Critique, reason legislates for itself in the interests of law and desire. Finally, in the *Critique of Judgment*, most notably in the sublime, there exists a "discordant accord" of the faculties, which are intended to produce harmony, but one faculty does not reign over all the others.[29]

For Deleuze, in the First Critique "only understanding legislates in the faculty of knowledge or in the speculative interest of reason."[30] Therefore, the functions of imagination and sensibility, along with Kant's conceptions of time and space and subjectivity or apperception all serve to (or are supposed to) uphold this legislative primacy of understanding. However, this reading of Kant in a Deleuzian light illuminates the tensions or discordances which are covered over by the "legislative primacy of understanding," specifically the resistance of imagination. Imagination occupies a more significant role in the First Critique than Kant is comfortable in granting, and yet he struggles to deny this insight.

Kant is constrained to check the importance and the scope of imagination because otherwise it will threaten the objectivity of determinative knowledge won by the understanding in the Transcendental Deduction. Deleuze points out that such a legislative victory by the understanding results in a fractured I because Kant has to divide the subject in order to ensure that understanding works properly. Only by separating and segregating the empirical I and the apperceptive I can Kant guarantee the objectivity of phenomenal knowledge. But this very separation, which plays itself out along the "line" of time Kant lays down in the Transcendental Aesthetic, fractures both the subject Kant establishes and eventually the determinative knowledge Kant desperately holds onto.

Deleuze, in each of the Kantian critiques, asks whether there is a "higher faculty" of knowledge, desire, and feeling.[31] This higher faculty relates to the supersensible, and occurs at that point where the faculties (as modes of knowing) surpass themselves and give voice to the unsurpassable itself. This happens paradigmatically in the *Critique of Judgment*, where it is the discordant accord of reason and imagination that pushes the faculties beyond themselves and gives rise to a higher faculty of feeling. "The sublime," Deleuze writes,

> brings the various faculties into play in such a way that they struggle against one another, the one pushing the other towards its maximum or limit, the other reacting by pushing the first towards an inspiration which it would not have had alone. Each pushes the other to the limit, but each makes the one go beyond the limit of the other.[32]

The existence of a "higher form" of a faculty of knowledge, desire, or feeling, suggests that the conflicts among the faculties are not only serious but also mobile and transitory. This Deleuzian view of a rearrangement of the relationships among the Kantian faculties allows the possibility of rereading the *Critique of Judgment* for insights into the fundamental conflicts among the faculties in the *Critique of Pure Reason*. Deleuze develops a language and a logic which allows a passage from the First Critique to the Third, and then back again to the First Critique. This passage follows a trajectory of semi-consistent faculties or powers such as imagination and understanding with the provision that such faculty-language is pragmatic and heuristic and should not be reified into static psychological entities.

Conclusion

By examining the Transcendental Analytic from the perspective of Deleuze, we have seen that time splits the Kantian subject into a passive self that appears as object of representation and an active self that performs the representing. This fracturing of the Kantian self by time via transcendental imagination works itself out in a powerful way in the Transcendental Schematism, which is where this reading of Kant is leading. First, however, I will return to the *Critique of Judgment*, in order to understand the status of imagination in the feeling of the sublime. In the Third Critique the faculties of imagination, understanding, and reason occupy different roles, and compose a different accord, one whose discord will ultimately rebound back into the First Critique. This relationship of imagination and understanding in the sublime is then read back into the *Critique of Pure Reason*, in a way which makes the problematic of this study, the negative power of imagination in the Schematism of the Pure Concepts of the Understanding, visible. Chapter Five therefore prepares the way for an explicit reading of the Schematism in the *Critique of Pure Reason* in Chapter Six.

5   The Analytic of the Sublime

Introduction

This chapter develops a reading of the sublime in Kant's *Critique of Judgment*, in order to show its impact on the *Critique of Pure Reason*. This reading follows Lyotard's in many respects, but also diverges, and adopts the spirit, if not all of the substance, of Derrida's essay "Parergon" from *The Truth in Painting*. The basic contention is that the sublime, understood as a problem concerning the negative imagination, represents the problem of the Schematism writ large. The reading of the sublime which I develop shatters externally, or from outside, the project of the First Critique, whereas the reading of the Schematism developed in the next chapter shatters the explicit project of the First Critique from the inside. The final chapter undertakes a theological evaluation of the status of the notion of the sublime which results in and from these shatterings.

I

Most interpreters of Kant stress the independence of the Third Critique from the First, whether the intent is to emphasize the architectonic whole of reason in which every element of each of the three critiques has a distinct place or, on the other hand, to secure an independent region for art and aesthetic feeling.[1] While the Third Critique cannot be amalgamated into the First, it cannot be completely divorced from it, either. At stake is the relationship between the general aesthetics of form set out in the Transcendental Aesthetic of the *Critique of Pure Reason*, and the specialized artistic aesthetic treated in the *Critique of Judgment*. What do these two different uses of aesthetics have to do with each other? My contention is that they cannot be separated, but more importantly, Kant's discussion of artistic aesthetics affects or deforms the general aesthetics of the pure forms of time and space according to a particular logic of supplementarity.

Derrida's notion of a supplement refers to a so-called artificial entity without which the more "natural" entity would not be what it is. In *Of*

Grammatology, Derrida analyzes writing, culture, or death as a supplement to speech, nature, or life in the work of Rousseau. According to Derrida, evil for Rousseau is an exterior addition to the natural goodness of humanity.[2] Nature's goodness should be self-sufficient, but the existence of evil represents a catastrophe which necessitates education as a substitute-supplement to Nature. All of culture, including writing, is an exterior addition, a supplement, whose existence also represents an accident or deviation from nature. What Derrida shows, however, is that "there is a lack in Nature and . . . because of that very fact something is added to it."[3] The supplement is unnatural but it comes about naturally through nature, that is, something in nature fails, and the supplement, culture, is necessary to substitute for it in order to correct it. Derrida questions the rigorous distinction between nature and culture in Rousseau, and he suggests that culture or evil already exists at the origin, the natural source, contaminating and corrupting it. This very corruption, however, allows both nature and culture to exist or occur at all.

Although conceived as derivative or secondary, a supplement can be found at the heart of what it supplements as the condition of possibility for its existence. As opposites, life depends on death to exist as life; death cannot be simply and purely excluded from life. The aesthetics of the *Critique of Judgment* supplement the aesthetics of the *Critique of Pure Reason*, but the First Critique is not a pure origin or aesthetics which is uncorrupted by the specialized aesthetics of artistic judgment. In the same way, the reflective judgment of the Third Critique, which is both subjective and involves a claim to universality, supplements and distorts the objective, determinate judgment of the First Critique, which is the model of theoretical judgment. Obviously, Kant does not present the aesthetics of the Third Critique as an evil deviation from a pure origin of aesthetics in the First Critique. What I am petitioning in this Derridean logic of supplementarity, however, is the confusion which results when Kant appears to subsume artistic aesthetics under the general universal aesthetics of the *Critique of Pure Reason*. At the same time, the special aesthetics explained in the *Critique of Judgment* undermine or threaten the very construction of a universal or "natural" aesthetics along with Kant's model of objective knowledge in the First Critique. A logic of supplementarity implies that the *Critique of Judgment* can be neither an advance beyond the *Critique of Pure Reason*, as if such a work makes the First Critique obsolete, nor a special case which can be comfortably set within an architectonic laid out by the First Critique, an example subsumed under a general rule or master plan. In some ways, then, this picture of the relation between the First and Third Critiques approaches Derrida's logic of exemplarity, developed in *The Other Heading*.[4] The particular example—aesthetics in the Third Critique—undermines or deconstructs the general rule—aesthetics in the

First Critique. The *Critique of Judgment* has to do with the *Critique of Pure Reason*, but in such a way that it radically deforms and distorts it, rather than leaving its integrity unchallenged.[5]

II

In the *Critique of Judgment*, as already stated in Chapter Three in the discussion of Lyotard, a judgment of beauty, or taste, is necessarily subjective, even though it involves the demand that it be universally communicable. Aesthetic judgments of taste lack an objective content, which means that they refer to experiences which cannot be subsumed under the categories of the pure concepts of the understanding. Aesthetic judgment consists in a disinterested pleasure taken in "the mere reflection on the form of an object."[6] The pleasure which arises in this way refers to the purposiveness of an object, which humans can relate to their own feeling of purposiveness in an analogical way. The objective basis, so far as it exists for a properly aesthetic judgment, is "the harmony of the form of the object with the possibility of the thing itself according to a prior concept of the thing that contains the basis of that form."[7] A judgment of taste involves a sense of the purposive form of an object without any actual content or objective purpose: "*Beauty* is an object's form of *purposiveness* insofar as it is perceived in the object *without the presentation of a purpose*."[8] Derrida calls the form of purposiveness finality, and the objective presentation of a purpose an end, and he writes that it is a finality *without* end which creates beauty for Kant. It is the pure cut of the "without [*sans*] that counts for beauty," because only the lack of a determinate end allows the free play of subjective form which allows a feeling of beauty to occur.[9]

In terms of the First Critique, the objective presentation of a purpose would be a content or concept which would possess objective validity, based on the Transcendental Deduction of the Categories. Why does an aesthetic judgment of beauty lack such objective content? The answer is that such aesthetic judgment consists in a "free play of the cognitive powers" of imagination and understanding.[10]

In his essay, "Kant's Explanation of Aesthetic Judgment," Dieter Henrich treats the "structure of the harmonious play" of understanding and imagination. He distinguishes between the determinative judgment of the First Critique and the reflective judgment of the Third. In the latter case, "imagination is responsible for the formation of perceptions," because reflective judgment progresses in the reverse direction of determinative judgment.[11] Rather than moving from categories to intuitions, reflective judgment proceeds from intuitions to categories. Reflective judgment holds the power of imagination (as it perceives and thus synthesizes a manifold) up to understanding in such a way that it stimulates a freedom of activity of imagination as it passes through manifolds and the production of forms. I agree with Henrich's account of aesthetic judgment, but I also question whether determinative judgment can be kept separate from such reflective judgment, or whether it operates in largely the same way. This claim becomes clearer in the next chapter, where I dismantle the objective and determinative interpretation of the Schematism, and read it more along the lines of the reflective judgment of the Third Critique. This play of the subject's cognitive powers, "where the understanding serves the imagination rather than vice versa," allows for the intuition of purposiveness in the form of an object, but it prevents the objective ascription of a conceptual purpose.[12]

Previously, when he wrote the *Critique of Pure Reason*, Kant believed that such an experience was not possible, that aesthetic feelings were purely and simply subjective, but he experienced a breakthrough to a critical "Critique of Taste" in 1787.[13] The price paid for this breakthrough, however, is the recognition of the status of imagination as an equal partner for the understanding, which prevents the objective application of the categories. The fact that the free play of understanding and imagination is "necessarily subjective" for Kant demonstrates the acuteness of the crisis of the deduction of the categories if imagination is there granted an independent role. The significance of imagination threatens the objective validity of any judgment, and thus the legislative integrity of the understanding, which if not carefully circumscribed troubles the deduction at the heart of the *Critique of Pure Reason*. This threat, that any exercise of imagination not subordinated to the activity of understanding results in a free play which is necessarily subjective and lacks objective content, motivates the rewriting of the Transcendental Deduction, also in 1787.

In turning from the beautiful to the sublime, it is important to remember that both are included under aesthetic judgment, and that a logic of supplementarity or exemplarity is again at work in this relationship. Unfortunately, many interpreters desire to bracket the sublime off from the realm of aesthetics, and consign it simply to morality, or want to dismiss it by subsuming it under artistic aesthetics as merely a special, if somewhat odd, case. Paul Crowther, in *The Kantian Sublime*, argues against this latter dismissal, or the neglect of Kant's discussion of the sublime in the "reception of Kant's aesthetics in the Anglo-American and German traditions of philosophy in the twentieth century." He goes on, however, to use the sublime to create an alternative, aesthetic morality free from the constraints of the First and Second Critiques.[14] On the other hand, Lyotard argues that the "sublime can be thought of as an extreme case of the beautiful" in which there occurs "the proliferation of forms by an imagination gone wild."[15] That is, any aesthetic judgment of beauty is capable of progressing to the infinite striving which marks the sublime. Kant writes that the distinction between the beautiful and the sublime consists in beauty being a perception of form of an object which represents it as being bound to that form. A sublime experience, on the other hand, has to do with "a formless object, insofar as we present *unboundedness*."[16] This unbounded-ness comes about as the result of a proliferation of forms by the imag-ination, according to Lyotard, and it results in a negative pleasure or contra-purposiveness. The sublime formlessness resists or breaks the form assigned to it in order to attribute purposiveness to it. But this negative experience results in a higher pleasure, because we realize that it is not the object, but our own mind, which stimulates the experience of the un-boundedness of the object.[17]

III

What are the dynamics of a sublime feeling or judgment? Kant claims that the sublime represents an interaction between imagination and reason. Imagination exchanges partners, forgoing the free play of beauty with the understanding in favor of what becomes a desperate struggle with reason which marks the sublime. In the *Critique of Judgment*, imagination leaves the understanding behind and enters into conflict with reason. As Kant explains:

> [What happens is that] our imagination strives to progress toward infinity, while our reason demands absolute totality as a real idea, and so [the imagination,] our power of estimating the magnitude of things in the world of sense, is inadequate to that idea. Yet this inadequacy itself is the arousal in us of the feeling that we have within us a supersensible power.[18]

Kant provides this explanation as part of what he calls the mathematical sublime, which he distinguishes from the dynamical sublime. The math-ematical sublime refers to our cognitive power, while the dynamical sub-lime refers to our power of desire. Connections can be made, therefore, between the mathematical sublime and the First Critique and the dynami-cal sublime and the Second Critique, but I want to resist a simple equation.

The mathematical sublime is much more fully developed than the dy-namical, and Kant's exposition of the dynamical sublime depends on the theoretical work he has done for the mathematical. Furthermore, magni-tude differs from might or power, but each involves an elevation or a progression "to infinity," that is, beyond the ability of a subject to be equal to it. Sublime magnitude is absolute magnitude, having no place on a scale of magnitude. The fact that sublime magnitude differs in kind from mathematical or theoretical magnitude makes it similar to power, where the might of nature cannot be calculated, only felt. In both cases, therefore, the sublime represents the aesthetic estimation of magnitude or power by a subject. Everything Kant says about the mathematical sublime can apply to the dynamical sublime, and vice versa. The distinction is the emphasis he lays on the experience. In the mathematical case, Kant focuses on the workings of imagination and reason in their complex interrelations. In the case of the dynamical sublime, however, Kant deals in a broad sense with the implications of the power of nature and its significance for human reason.[19] Since Kant is more explicit in his treatment of the mathematical sublime, it is easier to connect this discussion with the *Critique of Pure Reason*, from which Kant attempts to distinguish it.

A superficial reading of the difference between the mathematical sublime and the dynamical sublime might suggest that the mathematical sublime concerns the interrelationship among human faculties of reason and imagination in the presentation of an infinite idea. On the other hand, so an initial reading might continue, the dynamical sublime is distinguished because it represents the limit of human powers when confronted by the might of nature. Kant writes that "when in an aesthetic judgment we consider nature as a might that has not dominance over us, then it is *dynamically sublime*."[20] While the mathematical sublime attests to a conflict of the faculties of mind, the dynamical sublime shows the superiority of human dignity when it reflects upon nature's might from a safe distance, in a way that recalls Pascal's description of the human being as a "thinking reed." As correct as this reading may be, one should not be misled into thinking that the dynamical sublime has to do solely with external nature. As in the mathematical sublime, the characteristic of the dynamically sublime feeling or judgment "is contained not in any thing of nature, but only in our mind, insofar as we can become conscious of our superiority to nature within us, and thereby also to nature outside us."[21] Here Kant distinguishes religion from superstition, claiming that religion recognizes the source of sublimity inside the mind or subject, whereas superstition objectifies the source of the sublime outside the human being, whether as Nature or God. Kant claims:

> This alone is what intrinsically distinguishes religion from superstition. The latter establishes in the mind not a reverence for the sublime, but fear and dread of that being of superior might to whose will the terrified person finds himself subjected but without holding him in esteem; and this can obviously give rise to nothing but ingratiation and fawning, never to a religion based on good conduct.[22]

The crucial distinction between the dynamical and the mathematical sublime concerns the term elevation (*erheben*). In the dynamical sublime, imagination elevates the human being above nature's might, and raises humanity in its dignity above the threatening show of natural power. "Nature is here called sublime," Kant writes, "merely because it elevates our imagination, [making] it exhibit those cases where the mind can come to feel its own sublimity, which lies in its vocation and elevates it even above nature."[23] By focusing on the mathematical sublime, I want to call into question whether this elevation actually works, or whether the discord between reason and imagination initiated by the power of the negative imagination prevents such an elevation. For Hegelian idealism, elevation represents the core of *aufheben*, or the *Aufhebung*, where two antitheses are sublated and the resulting synthesis takes place at a higher level. The preservation of the essence of what has been sublated is what makes the sublime a sublimation, and this insight drives the Hegelian system, allowing Hegel to overcome the bifurcation in Kant between appearances and the thing-in-itself.[24]

Sublation builds upon elevation, which lifts up and preserves at a higher spiritual level. This is the positive power of imagination, which Heidegger finitizes, but in Hegel the positive power of imagination is infinite. On the other hand, in the mathematical sublime, an aporia is opened up which compromises such an elevation, and testifies to the power of a negative imagination to undo reason's constructive moral prospects.

My focus on the mathematical sublime, however, should not be understood as a dismissal of the dynamical sublime, along with its themes of power and might. In fact, the two cannot be completely separated, and in my treatment of the mathematical sublime, I introject power or might into the heart of the subject, already in the mathematical considerations of magnitude and temporality which manifest themselves in the First Critique. Another way to explain this procedure would be to say that this study of Kant represents the location of desire in the Kantian critical project, not in terms of the ethical will of the *Critique of Practical Reason*, but rather desire as power or might in the disturbing, negative power of imagination. This negative power of imagination is already at work in the mathematical sublime, and therefore already in the *Critique of Pure Reason*, as I will show.

IV

In order to return to an engagement with the Kantian text surrounding the inner workings of the imagination in the constitution of the mathematical sublime, I will detour via a critique of a significant contemporary interpreter of the Kantian imagination. In *Imagination and Interpretation in Kant: The Hermeneutical Import of the Critique of Judgment*, Rudolf A. Makkreel traces Kant's notion of imagination from his pre-critical use, through the First Critique, and into the *Critique of Judgment*, but he misses the importance of the sublime, and specifically reason's conflict with imagination. Makkreel wants to develop resources for a Diltheyian hermeneutics, which influences his constructive reading of Kantian imagination as a capacity to enable such a hermeneutics. This agenda is reflected in his conclusion: "by viewing the first *Critique* within the frame of reference supplied by the third *Critique*, we also see that the preliminary interpretations of reflective judgment can precede the explanative claims of determinant judgment."[25] Makkreel provides a somewhat simple-minded Heideggerian reading in which the imagination's ability to cooperate with understanding in forming reflective judgments is seen as more primordial than the determinative or objective judgment delineated in the *Critique of Pure Reason*. Makkreel ignores the central challenge which the Third Critique presents to the First Critique, understood as the consequences of the negative power of imagination at work in the Kantian sublime.[26]

In an essay on "Imagination and Temporality in Kant's Theory of the Sublime," Makkreel asserts that in the sublime judgment the power of imagination institutes a regress which suspends and transcends linear time. Makkreel argues that what cannot be done in the First Critique, that is, the presentation of a series in one exhibition, is accomplished by imagination in the sublime. "The regress of imagination does not annihilate time as such" as some critics have charged, but "suggests the possibility of negating the mathematical or linear form of time."[27] As I will discuss later in the chapter, the situation is not nearly as simple as Makkreel suggests. He ignores Kant's claim in the Third Critique that imagination is unable to comprehend what it apprehends, and therefore he presents imagination as a simple, straightforward power which can accomplish feats in the *Critique of Judgment* that it could not in the *Critique of Pure Reason*. Makkreel claims that "whereas apprehension relates unit to unit in the time sequence, aesthetic comprehension intuits multiple units of measure as coexistents in an encompassing measure of magnitude." But aesthetic comprehension is what is most problematic, if not impossible, in the sublime. Furthermore, Makkreel takes his only example of "the comprehension of multiplicity as a unity," a numerical series, straight from the First Critique, without demonstrating any explicit relationship between the two texts. Makkreel's Heideggerian finite transcendence in an elevation above linear time recalls Hegel's infinite transcendence in sublation. In fact, the negative power of imagination in the sublime ultimately undoes the linear time of the First Critique.

Returning to Kant's exposition of the (mathematical) sublime, he claims that imagination possesses a capacity "to progress toward infinity." An aesthetic estimation of magnitude (our actual experience), which Kant separates from a mathematical estimation of magnitude, "exhibits absolute magnitude to the extent that the mind can take it in in one intuition."[28] The intuition of an aesthetic absolute magnitude falls to a power of imagination, according to Kant. He charges that:

> imagination must perform two acts: apprehension (*apprehensio*), and comprehension (*comprehensio aesthetica*). Apprehension involves no problem, for it may progress to infinity. But comprehension becomes more and more difficult the farther apprehension progresses, and it soon reaches its maximum, namely, the aesthetically largest basic measure for an estimation of magnitude.[29]

Kant says that imagination can apprehend to infinity. We can imagine situations which outstrip our ability to comprehend them. In this case, "the logical estimation of magnitude progresses without hindrance to infinity," but what the imagination can apprehend it "cannot comprehend in one intuition."[30] The imagination has the capacity to "think the infinite as *a whole* [which] indicates a mental power that surpasses any standard of sense."[31]

Reason, however, cannot tolerate such a state of affairs. Reason, according to Kant, steps in and demands that the imagination comprehend this infinite in one intuition, which the imagination cannot do. "Reason," Kant says, "makes us unavoidably think of the infinite . . . as *given in its entirety* (in its totality)."[32] The inability of imagination to comprehend what it can apprehend is what leads to the element of displeasure in the sublime. The sublime is contra-purposive, because it conflicts with one's purposeful ability to represent it. The sublime judgment is still a pleasure, however, because it is not the object which propels the imagination beyond itself and at the same time demands its presentation in one idea, but a person's own reason. The purposiveness consists in the imagination's might being "still inadequate to reason's ideas."[33]

Reason prescribes a law to imagination, and demands that it comprehend its infinite apprehension in one intuition or presentation. Imagination's failure is then reason's success, because reason has the power to break the imagination and show up its inadequacy. Lyotard writes that

> the imagination does violence to itself in order to present a magnitude, which is a sign of an absolute order of magnitude (magnitude itself). Moreover, the imagination does violence to itself because reason has the strength to demand this of it.[34]

The imagination wounds itself in attempting to present absolute magnitude, but this failure is a success for reason and morality. A feeling of the sublime "that is beyond our ability to attain to an idea *that is a law for us* is RESPECT."[35] The displeasure which results from the failure of imagination results in a pleasure at the restoration of harmony and (moral) law. The conflict of imagination and reason is thus ultimately purposive, for Kant, because reason is able to reassert itself, and our fear and trembling in the face of our own inability to conceptualize the absolute magnitude of aesthetic experience turns into reassurance when we realize that it is the power of our own mind to progress to infinity and then to rein itself in which testifies to its might, rather than any object existing externally.

V

Can reason really contain the destructive power of imagination? In Kant's discussion of the mathematical sublime, reason steps in to harness the unbridled power of imagination to proceed to infinity in its apprehension of forms. In the brief description of the dynamic sublime, which I read as complementary to the mathematical, Kant suggests that humans make judgments about the sublime in nature when faced with its might. This might, however, "has no dominance over us" because although it arouses fear, nature is ultimately no match for the power of reason understood as human moral dignity.[36] We consider nature from a safe distance, and we judge that it has no power (at the moment) to harm us. This judgment of the impotence of nature does not mean that nature lacks the power to kill a person, but it testifies to the ability of human reason to estimate or take a reckoning of nature, and to pronounce judgments upon its worth and meaning. How is this judgment possible?

In the *Prolegomena to Any Future Metaphysics*, Kant spells out the implications of the *Critique of Pure Reason*, that the human understanding is able to discover laws in nature because they were initially placed there by the mind. Kant writes: "The understanding does not derive its laws (*a priori*) from, but prescribes them to, nature."[37] Therefore, "if in judging nature aesthetically we call it sublime, we do so not because nature arouses fear, but because it calls forth our strength" to determine the meaning of nature in the first place.[38] In the case of the Third Critique, however, nature is determined not by means of conceptual understanding, but by practical moral reason. Kant stresses that "a judgment about the sublime in nature requires culture," which "has its foundation in human nature ... namely the predisposition to the feeling for (practical) ideas, i.e., to moral feeling."[39] This predisposition to moral feeling governed by practical reason legislates in the special case of the sublime, in order to "save" moral interests or ends when they become threatened by the imagination's power to progress to infinity. In the dynamic sublime, of course, Kant argues that "nature is here called sublime merely because it elevates our imagination, [making] it exhibit those cases where the mind can come to feel its own sublimity."[40] This elevation of imagination, and the fear to which it gives rise, can be understood in two ways: by thinking the dynamical sublime in relation to Hegelian sublation, as I mentioned above, or by relating it to the detailed discussion of the mathematical sublime. In both cases, dynamical and mathematical, imagination progresses beyond its proper limits, whether conceived in terms of magnitude or power, and outstrips the ability of understanding to keep up, necessitating reason's intervention for the purpose of morality.[41]

Reason must preserve moral ends and contain the disturbing power of imagination, which threatens to overwhelm the subject. The question can be raised, however, whether Western culture retains the confidence in reason possessed by the European Enlightenment. On the contrary, does not the breaking out of irrational if not insane events such as two devastating world wars, the *Shoah*, and the brutal power of nuclear weapons to destroy life on earth call into question Kant's confidence in the ability of reason to contain the awesome and fearful power of imagination and direct it to moral and purposeful ends? John Sallis suggests that reason functions in the sublime as a kind of guardrail

> that protects and preserves precisely that self-disclosure that is achieved in the judgment of the sublime . . . The guardrail limits the spacing that commences as tremoring. It prevents one's ever decisively losing oneself in the abyss; it guarantees self-recovery, assures that self-disclosure is self-recovery.

Sallis asks the anachronistic question from Kant's point of view: "But what if now—today—such assurance were no longer available?"[42] Kant possessed an Enlightenment confidence in reason which many contemporary thinkers may lack.

According to Derrida, the distinctive aspect of the sublime is that it is framed. The frame, or *parergon*, separates the observer from the destructive in-breaking of nature or a human work of art. In his essay "Parergon," Derrida calls into question Kant's ability to keep the sublime safely within its frame. In this project, Derrida moves from the sublime object which is "almost unpresentable" because it is "almost too large," to the notion of the colossal, which in its prodigious monstrosity overflows or exceeds its final limit or concept, even the limitation called forth by reason to contain it.[43] The colossal bursts the frame which is constructed to contain it, and problematizes any attempt at representation, whether of a work of art or of an object in nature. "The sublime quality of the colossal," Derrida writes, "although it does not derive from art or culture, nevertheless has nothing natural about it. The cise of the colossus is neither culture nor nature, both culture and nature."[44] Although, for Kant, imagination and reason give rise to purposiveness by their conflict, and the might of nature is invigorating when it is considered from a safe distance, in the early twenty-first century the necessary distance supplied by the frame which sets humanity apart from nature is lacking, especially in an era of ecological or environmental crisis. One may also lack confidence that reason always comes out on top in its conflict with imagination, thus preserving harmony or purposiveness.

Paul de Man asks a similar question, albeit in a different way. For de Man, the inability of imagination to present the sublime object, despite its alliance with reason, undoes "the very labor of reason."[45] De Man attends to the positive power of the imagination as *Einbildungskraft*, or the ability to reproduce or represent. The sublime represents a failure of imaginative representation, understood as a "material disarticulation not only of nature but of the body . . . [which] marks the undoing of the aesthetic as a valid category. The critical power of a transcendental philosophy undoes the very project of such a philosophy."[46] I agree in broad terms with his conclusion, but I do not believe that it is a failure of *imagination* which brings this situation about. The breaking or destabilization of forms is brought about, not by the inability of imagination to perform its positive power, to give form to or to synthesize intuitions, but rather by the proliferation of forms of an imaginative power gone wild—as Lyotard notes—in a negative sense, which outstrips the ability of understanding to comprehend it, and (I suggest) punctures the ability of reason to constrain it. In the following chapter I will demonstrate in the *Critique of Pure Reason* the dynamics of this negative imagination which schematizes, or gives form, but in its very process of schematization prevents the reproduction or representation of such a form-giving. We have failed thus far, however, to ask the central question of the *Critique of Judgment*: why does the understanding disappear in the judgment of the sublime?

VI

Kant writes that

> just as the aesthetic power of judgment in judging the beautiful refers the imagination in its free play to the *understanding*, so that it will harmonize with the understanding's *concepts* in general . . . so in judging a thing sublime it refers the imagination to reason so that it will harmonize with reason's *ideas*.[47]

Why does the imagination leave the understanding behind when it progresses toward infinity? Is it not because the imagination outstrips the understanding's ability to conceptualize or comprehend? Lyotard claims that "the

Idea of an infinite magnitude . . . is off-limits for understanding. As we have said, the understanding cannot conceive of the unlimited, or even of the limit."[48] And yet, Lyotard does not develop the implications of the inability of understanding to conceive the unlimited.

In the *Critique of Pure Reason*, especially in the Transcendental Deduction of the second edition, rewritten in 1787, Kant is careful to eliminate the power of comprehension from imagination. This is the same power of comprehension which he claims the imagination is incapable of in the *Critique of Judgment*. In the first edition of the First Critique, Kant delineates three syntheses: apprehension, reproduction, and recognition. The synthesis of apprehension is the result of intuition, while imagination performs the synthesis of reproduction of the manifold of sensory intuition. Kant writes that the "synthesis of apprehension is thus inseparably bound up with the synthesis of reproduction" (A102). What he calls comprehension in the *Critique of Judgment*, Kant could refer to as reproduction or presentation by the pure productive power of imagination in the first edition of the *Critique of Pure Reason*. Even if this is the case, however, Kant is careful to separate the synthesis of recognition in a concept from the power of imagination as a separate faculty in the first edition, and he associates the synthesis of recognition with the transcendental unity of apperception.

In the second edition, furthermore, which Kant rewrites just before his breakthrough to his understanding of a "Critique of Taste," in 1787, Kant eliminates the middle synthesis of imagination, and assigns the figural synthesis of apprehension to the productive power of imagination. He describes that "synthesis of apprehension" as "that combination of the manifold in an empirical intuition, whereby perception, that is, empirical consciousness of the intuition (as appearance), is possible" (B160). Again, the synthesis of apprehension, "that is to say, perception" must conform to the categories of the pure concepts of the understanding (B162). "All synthesis, therefore, even that which renders perception possible, is subject to the categories" (B161).

It is helpful to remember that Kant, in the second edition Deduction, reduces the number of syntheses to two, a figurative and an intellectual synthesis. The transcendental synthesis of imagination belongs to sensibility, and can carry out only the figurative synthesis. The intellectual synthesis, however, "is carried out by the understanding alone, without the aid of imagination" (B152). Understanding conceptually produces the combination of the manifold for inner sense. Insofar as the synthesis of apprehension relates to sensory perception, and is subject to the categories, it cannot be anything other than a figurative synthesis. In this case, apprehension is properly the domain of the transcendental synthesis of imagination. Kant does not use the term comprehension in the second edition Deduction, but

if he did it would have to refer to the intellectual synthesis of the understanding. Now, the objective categories do not operate in the same way in
aesthetic judgments; their objectivity is compromised by imagination. I
have suggested that the objective validity of the pure concepts of the
understanding are compromised by the importance of imagination within
the *Critique of Pure Reason*. This conclusion can be grasped in light of
what Sallis calls "the erosion of the judgment in the judgment of taste."[49]
According to Sallis, "in the development of the theory of the sublime one
can discern, as with the judgment of taste, an erosion of the judgmental
structure that Kant places initially at the center of the judgment of the
sublime."[50] I suggest that this erosion has to do less with judgment in
general, than with the objectivity of the Kantian understanding. The free
play Kant tries to keep in check breaks out in desperate seriousness with
the sublime, resulting in a tremoring (*Erschütterung*) which eventually
extends beyond the *Critique of Judgment* to encompass the *Critique of
Pure Reason*.[51]

Kant enacts a sleight of hand. He backgrounds the importance of the
productive imagination in the second edition of the *Critique of Pure Reason*, while at the same time he highlights the inability or failure of imagination in the *Critique of Judgment*. What passes almost unnoticed in this
endeavor, however, is the vanishing act Kant performs on the understanding in the Third Critique. In the sublime, understanding is rendered completely impotent, because the power of imagination to apprehend to infinity
outstrips the ability of understanding to conceptualize, comprehend, and
present such an infinite apprehension as an intuition. To subsume an intuition under a concept, to comprehend, is the understanding's province and
task in the *Critique of Pure Reason*. In the *Critique of Judgment*, however,
Kant makes understanding vanish, and then blames the imagination for its
failure, that is, for the imagination's failure to perform what the understanding is properly supposed to perform. Kant is then constrained to
make aesthetic judgment a separate case of reflective judgment, despite the
existence of reflection already in the First Critique in The Amphiboly of
Concepts of Reflection, in order to preserve the determinative judgment
particular to the understanding in the *Critique of Pure Reason*. If reason is
unable, or even barely able to contain the disturbing and destructive power
of imagination, how much more impotent is Kant's vaunted power of
analytic understanding.

VII

This situation of a crisis of understanding which rebounds from the *Critique of Judgment* to the heart of the First Critique, is essentially a crisis of
time and subjectivity. In the *Critique of Pure Reason*, a linear temporality

constructs the self as an object of empirical intuition, while an active synthesis of time as transcendental unity of apperception makes such an intuition of self possible. As Deleuze perceives, however, locating time at the center of the self splits the self into active and passive components. This fissuring of time is related to the Kantian sublime, particularly Kant's description of the mathematical sublime.

The mathematical sublime represents the attempt by the imagination to present "comprehension in *one* intuition, and *exhibition* of all the members of a progressively increasing numerical series."[52] As Lyotard puts it, the imagination is placed under the demand by reason to "grasp . . . what is successive" "in one glance."[53] Since imagination fails at this task, reason declares victory and decrees ultimate purposiveness. The inability to "think the infinite as a whole," however, points rather to the breakdown of understanding. For Kant, understanding is that faculty which conceptualizes according to rules in the First Critique, and for understanding to work, that is, to be able to apply its categories to intuitions, it requires a linear successiveness of time. This linear succession allows the possibility of inner sense, which is required to bring order into experience. Kant's whole theory of time-determination relies on linear succession, or a notion of temporality in terms of a line, in order for experience to be meaningful in any objective way.

The sublime, however, represents the breakdown of the understanding, because the understanding is unable to conceptualize infinity aesthetically, that is, to and for a subject, even if it is able to conceptualize infinity abstractly or theoretically in mathematics. In fact, however, an aesthetic consideration already inhabits Kant's understanding of mathematics. For Kant, the equation $7 + 5 = 12$ is a synthetic judgment. This is the case because the sum must be synthesized by a subject, who cannot represent sensibly the progressive addition of $7 + 5$ in one intuition. The mathematical sublime represents the attempt to conceive an absolute magnitude, as opposed to the relative extensive and intensive magnitudes of the Axioms of Intuition and Anticipations of Perception (A162–76/B202–18). The attempt by a feeling subject, however, to conceive an absolute magnitude in one representation, undoes the linear temporality required by understanding, and results in what Lyotard calls "the destruction of temporality proper to all presentation."[54] Since time constitutes the Kantian subject in the *Critique of Pure Reason*, the "'regression' of imagination in sublime feeling strikes a blow at the very foundation of the subject."[55] Lyotard exposes the inter-workings of this dynamics of time in the sublime, but he does not fault the understanding, or appreciate to what extent the understanding is compromised in the First Critique. Lyotard follows Kant in considering the inability to make a presentation of an apprehension of infinity a wounding of imagination. "The imagination does violence to itself in order to present a magnitude," Lyotard writes, "which is a sign of the subjective absolute of magnitude (magnitude itself)."[56] Lyotard overlooks the violence already done to understanding, which Kant effaces because he cannot face the undoing of his theoretical system. Lyotard recognizes the inability of understanding to progress to the differend which occurs between reason and imagination in the sublime, but he does not realize the significance of the understanding's failure. The understanding must already have been violated, or rendered impotent in order for it to be unable to progress to the differend or conflict which marks the sublime. And this violence has already taken place in the *Critique of Pure Reason*.

Kant clearly assigns the function of apprehension in the First Critique to imagination. In apprehension of the manifold, "imagination has to bring the manifold of intuition into the form of an image" (A120). This activity, however, must be governed by the understanding, in order that such an image will conform to the rule of concepts, which as transcendental apperception requires a linear sequentiality:

> Only in so far, therefore, as I can unite a manifold of given representations in *one consciousness*, is it possible for me to represent to myself the *identity of the consciousness in* [i.e., throughout] *these representations*.
>
> (B133)

Understanding, according to Kant, produces the combination of the manifold for inner sense (B155). That is, understanding "determine[s] *inner sense* according to its form" (B155), and this inner sense *as it is produced*, has been defined in the Transcendental Aesthetic as linear and successive (B47), even if, as the universal condition for all appearances, time has only one unlimited dimension.

Time and the "I think" are one and the same, for Heidegger. That is, the transcendental unity of apperception represents the one unlimited dimension of time which gives form to and for inner sense. Heidegger emphasizes the importance of imagination in producing the inner sense, about which Kant remains ambivalent. Kant wants to constrain the imagination by the rule-giving conceptual categories of understanding, both to preserve the objectivity of empirical knowledge of phenomena, and also to prevent the imagination from running wild. The imagination has no problem apprehending to infinity, as Kant recognizes in the Third Critique.[57] As Lyotard notes, it is the proliferation of forms of an imagination gone wild which prompts the feeling of the sublime, rather than the inability of imagination to generate forms.[58] In the sublime, imagination outstrips understanding and its ability to keep up with imagination, even after the presence of imagination in a judgment of taste already rendered the objectivity of understanding invalid. Kant stages the drama of the conflict of imagination with reason in order to obscure the fact that it really represents a failure of understanding, both aesthetic and theoretical. The sublime reveals the negative power of imagination—not the inability of imagination to give form, but the disturbing ability of imagination to engender form beyond the ability of understanding to represent and reason to contain.

Deleuze demonstrates, as Lyotard ultimately recognizes, that the pure form of time and its relation to transcendental apperception splits the self into active and passive, and that this rupture runs through the *Critique of Pure Reason*. This fissure, I am arguing, is the same fissure Kant opens up in the sublime. Kant writes concerning "The Original Synthetic Unity of Apperception:"

> It must be possible for the "I think" to accompany all my representations; for otherwise something would be represented in me which could not be thought at all, and that is equivalent to saying that the representation would be impossible, or at least would be nothing to me.
>
> (B131–2)

The sublime is that which, although it is not quite nothing, and can almost be thought, cannot quite be thought, and is represented "in me" despite my inability to bring it to representation. This thinking of the sublime also seriously troubles the unity of the "I think," because I cannot represent clearly to myself this process of representation.

Conclusion

An analysis of the relationship among the Kantian faculties that make up the mathematical sublime demonstrates that imagination outstrips the ability of understanding to comprehend the infinite in terms of conceptual categories. The sublime judgment represents an extreme case of what is already present in the judgment of beauty, although in inchoate form, because the existence of imagination there, in a free play with understanding, renders beautiful judgments necessarily subjective. When read in light of the First Critique, the problem of an aesthetic (subjective) apprehension of infinity problematizes the workings of a determinative understanding which relies on a linear notion of time. The tremoring set off by the sublime extends to the center of the *Critique of Pure Reason*, and necessitates a rereading of the significance of the transcendental imagination in Kant's Schematism.

The problem of the sublime, in essence, is a problem of representation. Derrida writes concerning the "sublime quality of the colossal," that

It is, perhaps, between the presentable and the unpresentable, the passage from one to the other as much as the irreducibility of the one to the other. Cise, edging, cut edges, that which passes and happens, without passing, from one to the other.[59]

This aporia that Derrida describes metonymically represents the conflicts or differends among the faculties of reason, imagination, and understanding, as well as the passage from active to passive self, but it most directly addresses the problem of coming-to-representation, or representation itself. A language is lacking to express literally this process of thinking— what it means to signify or represent, either to ourselves or to others, which is why we are forced to use such anthropomorphic faculty-language. So even representation or discussion of the process of representation must remain metaphorical or metonymical, at least on some level. Kant most directly and succinctly addresses this problem of coming-to-representation in his brief chapter on The Schematism of the Pure Concepts of the Understanding, and it is to the Schematism that one must turn in order to grasp the ultimate significance of the sublime, as well as the coalescence of imagination, temporality and subjectivity in Kant's work.

6   The transcendental imagination

Introduction

Kant's brief chapter, "The Schematism of the Pure Concepts of the Under-standing," appears under the heading of the "Transcendental Doctrine of Judgment" in the *Critique of Pure Reason*. Judgment refers both to the determinative judgment Kant develops in the analytic of the First Critique, but also to the special cases of aesthetic and teleological (or what Lyotard calls reflective) judgment treated in the *Critique of Judgment*. This rela-tionship between the conceptions of judgment in the First and Third Cri-tiques is supplementary or exemplary, but keep in mind that even in the Third Critique Kant deals with a general notion of judgment. He does not entitle his work, "Critique of Aesthetic Judgment" or "Critique of Reflec-tive Judgment." The claim of the title as well as the book is to treat judgment in general, and this claim turns back upon the First Critique such that determinate judgment according to concepts becomes a special case of judgment in general (as Lyotard claims).

The most important aspect of this complexity is that it works both ways. On the one hand, judgment seems to be treated in a general way as part of human knowing in the *Critique of Pure Reason*, such that aesthetic judgment in the Third Critique must be seen as a special case. On the other hand, judgment in general seems to be the realm of the Third Critique, and then the judgment operative in pure reason appears as a restricted exam-ple. In both cases, however, judgment is central to human knowing.

I

In order to make a judgment, according to the *Critique of Pure Reason*, one must subsume something under a rule (A132/B171). This activity of subsuming under rules is what Kant calls Schematism. Schematism refers to the procedure by which an intuition is related to a category of the understanding. Kant expresses this procedure by saying that "an object is contained under a concept" (A137/B176). Intuitions are purely empirical, whereas concepts lack any application to empirical objects; therefore Kant requires a method for the relation of these two separate entities, concepts and intuitions. A schematized concept is a concept which can be used.[1]

In order to relate concepts and intuitions, or to subsume intuitions under concepts, imagination is required. Kant declares that "there must be a third thing, which is homogeneous on the one hand with the category, and on the other hand with the appearance, and which thus makes the application of the former to the latter possible" (A138/B177). This "third thing," or "mediating representation," is called the transcendental schema. A schema is a product of imagination, specifically the transcendental imagination. "The schema is in itself always a product of imagination" (A140/B179). The power of mediating intuitions to concepts, however, is carefully assigned by Kant to understanding rather than imagination, in the same way as in the Transcendental Deduction. The "schematism of understanding effects . . . the unity of all the manifold of intuition in inner sense" "by means of the transcendental synthesis of imagination" (A145/B185). Nevertheless, imagination occupies a central place in human judging and knowing.

Kant attempts to clip the wings of imagination in order to preserve the sovereignty of understanding, but he cannot do away with his awareness of the importance of imagination at crucial locations within his system. One response to this situation could be to smooth over the wrinkles, grant imagination an equal status with understanding, and proclaim that all is well. Unfortunately, this result overlooks the struggle between imagination and understanding which breaks out violently in the sublime. This differend (Lyotard) exists already within the *Critique of Pure Reason*, but it is almost invisible because Kant has attempted to efface it. One is tempted, as many interpreters have done, either to take Kant at his word that judgment in the First Critique is subsumption under a rule, and dismiss the Third Critique as whimsical and subjective, or else celebrate the free play of the *Critique of Judgment* as more open-ended and democratic.[2]

This conclusion ignores two crucial points, both of which attest to the indeterminateness of judgment and understanding in the *Critique of Pure Reason*. Despite Kant's use of words like subsumption and rule, he admits that "judgment is a peculiar talent which can be practiced only, and cannot be taught" (A133/B172). Even more striking is his claim that "this schematism of understanding . . . is an art concealed in the depths of the human soul, whose real modes of activity nature is hardly likely ever to allow us to discover, and to have open to our gaze" (A141/B180–1). In his commentary, H.J. Paton strongly distinguishes subsumption from the activity of the transcendental imagination. "I see no trace of such a usage [of subsumption] in the chapter on Schematism," he writes.[3] So one must not simply assume that judgment in general, and schematism in particular, is a straightforward, ordered, determinate process. In fact, Schelling asserts that the "schema . . . is not a presentation determinate in all its aspects, but merely an intuition of the rule whereby a specific object can be brought forth. It is an intuition, and so not a concept, for it is that which links the concept with the object."[4] I argue below that while a schema is *intuitive*, it is neither simply an intuition nor a concept.

The first point to be stressed is that a schema is not a thing. It represents an act or an activity, a rule or procedure, but it is above all a dynamic process.[5] More specifically, schematism refers to the activity or process, while a schema refers to a product of this process. In this sense, a schema could be called a "thing," but it is a thing whose status is very strange. In his book, *The Transcendental Imagination*, Charles E. Winquist says that "the schema is the procedure of imagination in providing an image for a concept."[6]

A schema is not a thing in any ordinary sense because it is not an image, which is the second crucial distinction to be made. Kant claims that "the schema has to be distinguished from the image," because it is a "unity in the determination of sensibility" (A140/B179). This means that a schema represents a general image, for which Kant gives the example of a number, a thousand, whose "image can hardly be surveyed and compared with the concept" (A140/B179), because we cannot represent a thousand points in a line all at once. Therefore, a procedure or a pattern is required in order to give representation to "a universal procedure of imagination in providing an image for a concept," which is called the schema (A140/B179–80).

An image remains tied to sensibility, while a schema abstracts from sensibility in order to be able to represent a succession too great for sensible (or aesthetic) intuition to present in one unified representation. Kant's language here recalls the *Critique of Judgment*, where imagination is unable to comprehend a successive series in one glance. In the First Critique the transcendental imagination, under the control of the understanding, apparently is able to make a presentation of such a succession in a single representation or schema. When we represent the number five to ourselves, we can easily (according to Kant) picture five successive points on a line, which means that we are still in the realm of sensible intuition. But if we progress to a number as large as a thousand, we cannot hold together that many points in one representation empirically in our mind. We require, therefore, a procedure to encompass and represent a large magnitude in a unified presentation in order to conceive it distinctly. J. Michael Young writes that

> when we use a particular collection of sensible things to construct the concept of a certain quantity or magnitude, Kant calls that collection an *image (Bild)* of the concept in question. The general procedure, on

the other hand, by which we identify this or any collection as a collection of that quantity, and which therefore constitutes a sort of template of the concept in question, he calls the *schema* of that concept.[7]

A person cannot image a schema. Kant requires the transcendental schemata in order to relate sense intuitions to pure concepts, but we cannot sensibly represent to ourselves these schemata, much less the Schematism in itself. No concept is valid or applicable unless and until it is schematized, that is, related to sensible intuitions. "Although the schemata of sensibility first realise the categories," Kant argues, "they at the same time restrict them, that is, limit them to conditions which lie outside the understanding, and are due to sensibility" (A146/B186). Schemata actualize the categories of the understanding, but they render the determinateness of the understanding suspect, because they cannot be empirically represented. The fact that a schema is not an image means that the Schematism is itself indeterminate, that is, it is a process of representing or knowing which cannot itself be represented. Imagination (*Einbildungskraft*) makes possible synthesis in general, or knowing in general, but this power of imagination to give form lacks a determinate form.

In distinguishing an image from a schema, Kant states that

> the *image* is a product of the empirical faculty of reproductive imagination; the *schema* of sensible concepts, such as figures in space, is a product and, as it were, a monogram, of pure *a priori* imagination, through which, and in accordance with which, images themselves first become possible.
>
> (A141–2/B181)

It is telling that Kant uses the term "monogram" to describe the schema. Paton explains that "a monogram is now commonly regarded as a series of letters so interwoven as to constitute a whole . . . but there is an older usage in which 'monogram' meant a sketch or outline, and Kant himself seems to use it in this sense."[8] Later in the *Critique of Pure Reason*, Kant claims, regarding the "products of imagination," that "each is a kind of *monogram*, a mere set of particular qualities, determined by no assignable rule, and forming rather a blurred sketch drawn from diverse experiences than a determinate image" (A570/B598). This sentence supports Paton's argument that a schema is a "wavering" sketch or image.[9]

On the one hand, a schema understood as a wavering or blurry image prevents a full or adequate representation of it. Such "imagery" reinforces the notion that the schema represents a dynamic process that is the result of an activity of schematic imagination. On the other hand, I also want to retain the ordinary meaning of monogram as an interwoven combination of letters because it accords with my reading of the mathematical sublime. The succession of letters cannot be represented in and as a whole without sacrificing sensible clarity, because the presentation of a succession in one representation disrupts full and complete representation. Complete representation is impossible because Kant requires a linear succession of time in order for the understanding to function. Imagination works by synthesizing temporality into immediacy, but this process is itself dynamic, and thus incapable of being represented.

Heidegger passes over the distortion which the distinction between schema and image entails. He argues that a schema is merely a "pure image" which "belongs necessarily to transcendence." My argument is that Heidegger fails to appreciate the negative power of the schematism and the transcendental imagination, in part because he fails to take seriously enough the Third Critique.[10]

II

I have attempted to show that schema and schematism, far from being determinate categories of understanding, are in a certain sense indeterminate and related primarily to imagination. In the *Critique of Judgment*, Kant contrasts schemata with symbols in the course of his discussion of "Beauty as the Symbol of Morality." He claims that intuitions that are pure concepts of the understanding "are called schemata."[11] Symbols, on the other hand, are intuitions related to the ideas of reason. Here Kant uses the term *hypotyposis* or exhibition rather than judgment to refer to the making sensible of a concept or idea, but one could also use the terms presentation or representation as long as his conceptual distinctions are kept in mind. He divides *hypotyposis* into two types, "*schematic or symbolic*."[12] Both schematic and symbolic presentations are intuitive rather than discursive presentations. The difference between symbols and schemata, according to Kant, is that "schemata contain direct, symbols indirect, exhibitions of the concept. Schematic exhibition is demonstrative. Symbolic exhibition uses an analogy."[13] Here symbols appear indirect, ambiguous and indeterminate, while schemata appear direct and determinate.[14]

The fact that a schema is not an image, however, renders it less determinate and direct. A schema makes an exhibition or presentation, but it cannot itself be represented fully. In fact, an understanding of schematism more explicitly along the lines of imagination understands a schema as similar to a symbol. Both symbols and schemata are intuitive rather than discursive: "the intuitive [element] in cognition must be contrasted with the discursive [i.e., conceptual] (not the symbolic)."[15] Kant stresses that both are hypotyposes or exhibitions, "not mere characterizations, i.e., designations of concepts by accompanying sensible signs."[16] In contrasting the discursive element in cognition with the symbolic, Kant is making Tillich's noted distinction between sign and symbol, where a symbol, being intuitive, participates in that to which it points, while a sign, being discursive, does not.[17] Here both schemata and symbols are intuitive; neither is discursive, and this characterization implies that a schema can be thought of as a special case of intuitive symbol.

A schema is a special class of symbols, which relates more to understanding and imagination than to reason. Both symbols and schemata are intuitive rather than discursive, that is, they are intimately connected to experience. Schemata appear more determinate and direct, but this appearance is deceptive unless we keep in mind the fact that schemata are the result of a dynamic process which cannot be known completely. Kant wants to render schemata determinate and objective for the sake of our knowledge of phenomenal objects, while symbols express what cannot be known as an object of experience. The breakdown of the understanding (in that such schemata cannot be represented) suggests, however, that schemata are indeterminate, ambiguous, and open, at least in a formal sense, even if schematized representations seem more concrete. A schema is a special form of symbol, dealing with the process of understanding mediated through the transcendental imagination.

Kant claims that symbolic exhibition is analogical, and that

> judgment performs a double function: it applies the concept to the object of a sensible intuition; and then it applies the mere rule by which it reflects on that intuition to an entirely different object, of which the former object is merely a symbol.[18]

Kant says here that judgment applies a "mere rule," which undercuts the objectivity of his profligate use of the word rule in the schematism chapter. In any case, I would argue that judgment performs a similar double function in the schematism of imagination or understanding, only that the "entirely different" object to which it applies the rule is merely the same object at a different time. This temporal displacement, however, disrupts the unity of the perceived object, which Kant desperately tries to retain. One could understand analogical symbols along the lines of a metaphorical substitution, where the object lies on a different plane, whereas schemata function metonymically in a substitutively displacing process immanent in thinking an object apparently more directly, but with no less complexity. In this way the categories of understanding are generated by a process of schematism, which is the result of the working of the transcendental imagination, rather than static entities which organize intuitive experience in a hierarchical manner.

This insight into the schematic nature of knowledge, its production by transcendental imagination and its close connection with symbolic knowledge, also raises the question whether not only the concepts of the understanding but also the ideas themselves are schematized as symbols. That is, the negative or sublime imagination in its production of schemata, gives rise immanently to the ideas of self, world, and God which are later hypostasized into ideas of reason, which function as master symbols. Even though they function in a regulative rather than constitutive manner for Kant, the ideas of transcendental philosophy cannot lack any content whatsoever, nor any connection with empirical experience. The tentative conclusion, therefore, is that the ideas which give rise to paralogisms, antinomies, and theologies of pure reason are themselves generated by a schematism which can be marked but not fully understood.

III

The consequences of the dynamic nature of the Schematism have not yet been fully appreciated. This procedure, while allowing representation to occur, does not allow itself to be fully represented. The Schematism is the transcendental imagination, although Kant desires to appropriate the power of this transcendental imagination for the purposes of the understanding. A schema is not an image, and cannot be represented, except perhaps in a blurred or wavering manner. According to Kant, then, we can represent objects, but we cannot represent our own process, power, or ability to represent.

Referring to the "epistemological conception of the transcendental imagination," Winquist writes that "to understand the significance of the transcendental imagination, the mind would have to have an immediate knowledge of itself as it contributes to the total act of knowing."[19] The immediate knowledge of itself as a "total act of knowing" is impossible for the transcendental imagination, but as a demand it is a condition for knowing in general. This inability to represent our power of representation is therefore an epistemological wound inflicted by the transcendental imagination, understood in its negative sense. Humans possess the ability to represent objects, but they lack the ability to represent fully their own powers of representation, according to Kant. In *The Transcendental Imagination*, the development of an epistemological imagination into an ontological imagination by way of Heidegger and Whitehead, and finally into a hermeneutical theology, does not thereby overcome the power and importance of the epistemological imagination. In fact, Winquist reinscribes the epistemological imagination into Heidegger and Whitehead, as well as into theology itself.

The ability to represent objects cannot be completely separated from the inability to represent the ability to represent objects. The inability to represent, or to give form to, the process of representation, also affects the representation or knowing of any particular object. The inability (by the understanding) to represent the transcendental imagination—which is what makes representation possible—is an epistemological wound because it is representation—of intuitions by means of categories of the understanding—which makes knowledge possible for Kant. This affecting or infecting of the status of all human knowledge is a radical negativity understood as the effects of the transcendental imagination, and suggests the breakdown of the Kantian understanding in the determinative sense in which it is set up, although certainly not the inability to understand at all.

Imagination as the process or activity of representation disrupts the ability to represent and understand in any total sense. The negative (transcendental) imagination indicates not the inability to give form on the part of the faculty of imagination but rather, in its proliferation of temporal forms (as Lyotard recognizes), disrupts an understanding of this process (and thus of all our knowledge). The proliferation of forms by the productive imagination prompts a dizziness or disorientation, which is the result of a dynamic process in which the problem is not a lack but rather an excess of form. The activity of giving form (to objects or experiences) exceeds the capacity of human thinking to contain or represent it, and bursts the frame or *parergon* which attempts to locate, contain, and make safe representation. This negative imagination is the motor which drives Kant's critique(s).

IV

The process of representation, or the transcendental imagination, is both time-determining and also subject-determining. According to Kant, "time is contained in every empirical representation of the manifold. Thus an application of the category to appearances [the schematism] becomes possible by means of a transcendental determination of time" (A139/B179). According to Heidegger, time and the "I think" are the same, that is, the essence of the transcendental unity of apperception is temporality, and "time is the schema-image and not just the form of intuition which stands over against the pure concepts of the understanding."[20] Given the intimate affinity of temporality and subjectivity in Kant's philosophy, transcendental imagination, which effects experience as a determination of time (when employed by the conceptual understanding), is essentially the transcendental unity of apperception.

I am willing to go so far as to claim, with Heidegger, that the transcendental imagination *is* the transcendental unity of apperception, associating apperception more closely with imagination than understanding. Even if the two cannot be identified, they do share a structural similarity. Imagination mediates but also disrupts the relation of intuitions to concepts. The transcendental unity of apperception mediates between two selves, the empirical or phenomenal and the moral or noumenal, but ultimately it also disrupts their unity or identity. Imagination is a third between intuitions and concepts, homogeneous with each, but also strikingly heterogeneous to both. Of the transcendental schema, Kant writes: "Obviously there must be some third thing, which is homogeneous on the one hand with the category, and on the other with the appearance, and which thus makes the application of the former to the latter possible" (A138/B177). Just as obviously, the transcendental schemata must be different from categories as well as appearances, in order to be able to mediate or relate them in any way. This middle term, as the condition of relation of the two stems of thinking, intuitions and concepts, cannot be a third "thing" in any ordinary sense of the word. We do not possess three equal faculties or modes of thinking. The third is a tentative, shadowy term of relation which possesses no static existence in its own right. Apperception likewise is a third "self" between two selves, not exactly a third thing, but a relation which makes possible the other two which it relates, yet at the same time it holds them distinctly apart from one another in a kind of tension or polarity.

In his *Systematic Theology*, Tillich relies on polarities or "polar relations" such as "individuality and universality, dynamics and form, freedom and destiny," in order to explicate the "ontological structure" of his theology.[21] These polarities are not opposites, although Tillich emphasizes the tension between them more so than any middle or mediating term. Kant's transcendental imagination and/or transcendental apperception represents such a mediating term, but it poses deep problems for the structure of Kantian philosophy as a whole. Such middle terms cannot simply mediate between polarities in the construction of an identity, in a Hegelian sense. Rather, these very mediating processes fracture or problematize the identity of the very entities they bring together, as Deleuze has shown. Identity or subjectivity is not simple or immediate for Kant, but it is fractured and mediated by the processes which make it what it is.[22] Writing about Derrida, Rodolphe Gasché coins the term infrastructure to designate an "original synthesis" or "intermediary discourse," but these syntheses "cannot be seen as third terms that eventually initiate solutions in the form of speculative dialectics. Rather, these original syntheses ... are analogous to what in traditional philosophy, especially in Kant, has been relegated to transcendental imagination." Gasché also claims that the infrastructure "must be understood as the *medium of differentiation* in general," which suggests affinities with both Derrida and Deleuze.[23]

Temporality is what makes absolute identity impossible. The process of knowing or representing takes place in time. The very activity which determines objects as experiences within time can only be known in temporal terms. As already discussed, Kant uses the example of number when discussing the transcendental schema. Five can be represented by an image, but a thousand requires a schema, because we cannot fully represent to ourselves a thousand points at one time. The "universal procedure of imagination" provides a special kind of image which allows the use of this concept (A140/B179). The procedure the imagination must perform is to allow human thinking to represent a great magnitude of successive numbers or points in one presentation. "Every sensation has a degree of magnitude" (A143/B182), which means that the "schema of reality . . . is just this continuous and uniform production of that reality in time" (A143/B183). Kant treats schemata of possibility, actuality, and necessity, but "the schema of each category contains and makes capable of representation only a determination of time" (A145/B184). Here the imagination is ostensibly able to perform its task, to synthesize a temporal magnitude into one presentation, with the aid of the understanding.

How can the imagination's alleged impotence be understood, then, in the sublime, except by claiming that the *understanding* is unable to direct and constrain the power of imagination, thus letting it spin out of control? The Kantian understanding, however, is not able to perform its task completely even in the schematism of its categories, because it is forced to sacrifice the clarity of its representations, which become blurred or wavering. This inability of understanding to represent schemata as images or clear and precise representations attests to a sublime aspect of all knowing. Sublimity is a transcendental condition for the possibility of representing an object, because in order for the procedure of representation in conceptual understanding to work (determinately), it requires a linear, ordered, succession of time. On the other hand, the very temporality of the knowing process displaces the representing which it allows to occur. (Re)presentation or exhibition is a temporal concrescence, to use Whitehead's term, which gathers together or synthesizes an object or experience as a determination of time.[24] This process, however, also takes place within time, and therefore never equals itself or allows full and complete representation because that would freeze or fix the dynamic process.

Time occupies a central role in Kant's philosophy, connected as it is with imagination and subjectivity. In his *System of Transcendental Idealism*, which combines the subject material of Kant's three critiques into one book, Schelling explains that as a transcendental determination of time, the schema is "an intermediary between inner and outer sense."[25] Time mediates between inner and outer experience as space does not, so that "from the standpoint of reflection, time is merely a form of the intuition of inner sense," while "from the standpoint of intuition, on the other hand, time at the outset is already an *outer* intuition."[26] Schelling concludes that "this property of time, whereby it appertains at once to both inner and outer sense, is the sole ground for its role as the universal link between concept and intuition, or as transcendental schema."[27]

The distinction between inner and outer refers, metaphorically, to the distinction between the ability to represent objects in time as external appearances, and the need to refer that process of representation in meaningful, i.e., temporal, terms, to an inner act of intuition. The more one attempts to seize time from the inside, however, the more one is unable to grasp it. We can understand objects as they appear in time, but we cannot understand the capacity to envision or constitute experiences—the manifold—temporally.

The passage of time and human inability to conceive it in itself, prevent self or substance from being equal to itself—our experiences differ, because they are always temporally deferred. One can stand within experience and point to transcendental conditions of its possibility, but every grasping for the noumenal is in some respect phenomenal or empirical, which means that the noumenal cannot be known as such. Schematism or transcendental imagination, as the name for this process of thinking and representing, must be posited or thought but cannot be known.[28] Human beings (also) exist as determinations of time, as finite beings, and thus the attempt to arrest the act of thinking is never fully successful, because the act itself is temporal and gives time or distributes temporal effects (distributes our empirical selves as an empirical effect). In Deleuzian terms, time is off its hinges, in that it is no longer subordinate to movement, but time itself is the hinge or jointure of the self.[29]

V

This notion of schematism as time-determining is similar to Derrida's notion of *différance*. In his essay, "Différance," Derrida explains that "*différance* is literally neither a word nor a concept."[30] He invents this neologism by substituting an "a" for the "e" in the word difference (in French, *différence*). Derrida suggests two senses of the verb *différer*, each of which is operative in his term. First of all, to differ is to defer, for which Derrida uses the word *temporization*. *Temporization* means not only temporalization but also spatialization, that is, the dynamic "becoming-time of space and the becoming-space of time."[31] The other sense of *différer* is the familiar meaning of being not identical or dissimilar, that is, different. The notion of difference as non-identity is the common meaning of *différence*. What Derrida adds to this conception, which is captured by the "a" which can be written but not heard, is the idea of *temporization* or active deferral. The translator notes that "*différence* (in French) does not convey the sense of active putting off, of deferring (*différance* in what

would be its usual sense in French, if it were a word in common usage)."
The point is that Derrida's introduction of a new meaning hinges on the
idea of active deferral or *temporization*, which resembles the working of
the Kantian transcendental imagination.[32]

In *Of Grammatology*, Derrida analyzes Saussure's system of linguistic
signs, in which "the differential character of the sign" is "the foundation
of general semiology."[33] Saussure argues that signs are defined not by their
resemblance to what they represent, but by their differences from each
other in a system of language. Saussure emphasizes the synchronic or static
meaning of linguistic signs as they divide into signifier and signified. This
synchronicity becomes a structuralism which ignores the diachronic, or
temporal aspects of language.[34] Derrida, in his reading of Saussure, sets the
linguistic system in motion, suggesting that an active temporal flow of
language prevents the structures of sign systems from ever equaling each
other. In *Of Grammatology*, Derrida usually calls this process "spacing,"
but this word connotes "the articulation of space and time," where time
and space are joined in a dynamic becoming which Derrida calls *temporization* in "Différance," or *arche-writing* in *Of Grammatology*.[35] Derrida
uses Saussure's concept of the "arbitrariness of signs" to refer to the fact
that there exist a finite number of signs, but they indefinitely circulate in a
temporal process, such that each grasping of a sign in a concept freezes or
fixes it, and also distorts it. This distortion, which Derrida calls by different names to prevent ossification, is related to the process of the Kantian
transcendental imagination, which also disrupts a certain mode of human
knowing or signifying.

The indeterminacy of signs is built in, structurally, by means of a process of becoming internal to the sign itself. We can illuminate this at-times
mysterious process by means of our analysis of the Kantian schematism. In
order to relate Derrida's "concept" of *différance* to Kant's transcendental
imagination, I am making a structural analogy between Kantian representation and Derridean processes of signification. The schematism or the
transcendental imagination refers to the process of representation or signification which itself cannot be represented, because it differs from itself at
every moment. This process differs from itself because it is constantly
being deferred, and attempts to grasp or fix it always fall short because it
never ceases to move and generate new meanings. Derrida criticizes a
straightforward linear temporality in *Of Grammatology*, and problematizes
Kant based "on the concept of the line which so often intervenes in the
Kantian critique."[36] Derrida makes a similar critique to Bergson's, charg-
ing that Kant's discussion of time is too simplistic or what Bergson would
call spatial, but in contrast to Bergson, Derrida shifts terms, privileging
space rather than time. What is important for both Derrida and Kant is
that time and space cannot be easily separated, that both possess active

dynamic components, and that both refer to a process which cannot be seized by human thinking. Derrida makes spacing an active term, and privileges writing over speaking, but he is still grappling with the same problem, according to this reading. The active process of deferral or play of signs cannot be captured in a representation of a linear temporality, signified by a line.

Derrida claims that "such a play, *différance*, is thus no longer simply a concept, but rather the possibility of conceptuality, of a conceptual process and system in general."[37] This Kantian language refers to the conditions of possibility of signification, or what I have been calling representation. The dynamic flow of meaning necessitates that Derrida use different words to capture (obliquely) this process, which is why he claims that "there will be no unique name" or master word, not even *différance*.[38] For this reason, there are also no natural sharp distinctions between terms, but rather they merge into each other with what appears to be a wavering blurriness, but which is actually a disorienting complexity. Derrida attempts to express the inexpressible, which is the definition of the sublime. *Différance* exhibits, through a "pyramidal silence of the graphic signifier," what cannot be "exposed" or expressed, but only traced.[39] The process itself leaves traces, which are all of our concepts and signs.

Derrida's preoccupation with language leads him to emphasize the process of linguistic signification over the representation of objects, which is Kant's main concern. In a critique of Husserl (as well as Kant), Derrida suggests the possibility of a "new transcendental aesthetic" which would not remain "subjected to the instance of the living present, as [well as] to the universal and absolute form of experience."[40] This "universal and absolute form of experience" is experience conceived universally as an experience of an object by a subject. Derrida does not want to dismiss the concept of experience, only to redefine or widen it by means of textual, written, and indirect experiences, and ultimately experiences that burst our frames of understanding of what we perceive and define as experiences.

For a Derridean semiology, a Kantian intuition is an empirical experience of a linguistic signifier, while a sign itself resembles a Kantian concept, and finally, *différance* is the transcendental imagination or schematism. In *The Trespass of the Sign*, Kevin Hart argues that Derrida and Kant are engaged in a similar project of both exposing the necessary illusions of metaphysics and also delineating the conditions of possibility for metaphysics. "Just as Kant formulates 'necessary conditions of possible experience' so too Derrida establishes the 'general text' as the condition of possibility for the act of interpretation."[41] I am suggesting that although our philosophical framework has changed, the basic epistemological problem of knowing how it is we know—representation, signification, framing, exhibition, *Einbildungskraft* as the giving of form to experience, etc. (there is no one term)—remains.

Conclusion

My reading of the schematism is made possible by means of a detour through the sublime in the *Critique of Judgment*. An understanding of the sublime, however, when redirected back into the *Critique of Pure Reason*, exposes the workings of the transcendental imagination which is already operating in the First Critique. Understood in terms of a disrupting or fissuring negative imagination, the Kantian schematism reads very much like the Derridean (non)concept of *différance*, although it also has strong affinities with a Deleuzian (repetition of) individuation or differentiation.[42]

What are the theological implications of isolating a sublime moment for all representing, thinking, or knowing? I have argued that this reading of Kant is theological, at least in a formal way. What would it mean to work out a postmodern theology of the sublime? In the final chapter, I will articulate a tentative and constructive vision of a sublime theology which points out some suggestive connections and asks where theological thinking can be productive. In some ways, such a theology is necessarily a negative theology, in the sense of lacking a determinate or objective (Christian) content. On the other hand, by grappling with the forms of thinking itself, theological thinking can develop insights which are themselves sublime.

7 Towards a theology of the sublime

Introduction/Summa

A Kantian aporia presents itself within phenomenal experience, despite Kant's best efforts to circumscribe this situation and to save knowledge of appearances by cutting off access to things in themselves. I have enacted this problem by dramatizing the relations of the Kantian faculties of understanding, imagination, reason, and intuition. The disappearance of the understanding in the Kantian sublime testifies to its ultimate failure even within the First Critique, and inaugurates a desperate struggle between reason and imagination (which Lyotard calls a differend), from which struggle I have attempted to cast doubts on whether reason necessarily emerges victorious.

By reading the drama of the sublime back into the *Critique of Pure Reason*, I have shown that the (phenomenal) objectivity of the understanding is already compromised by its interaction with imagination. The importance of the transcendental imagination in the Transcendental Deduction but especially the Schematism problematizes an understanding based on linear time, revealing a dynamic process which gives time as the effect or form of experience. This temporality constructs subjectivity, but it also deconstructs any total and complete knowledge of this process and therefore of the subject or the source of time determination. The only understanding we can have of this process is indirect.[1] Finally, I argue that an understanding of this Kantian aporia is theological, because it pressures our thinking and knowing in transcendental ways.

I

For the early Heidegger of *Being and Time* and *Kant and the Problem of Metaphysics*, *Dasein* is a fundamental category because it offers an opening to the problem of Being itself. "Nevertheless," Heidegger concludes in *Being and Time*, "our way of exhibiting the constitution of Dasein's Being remains only *one way* which we may take. Our aim is to work out the question of Being in general."[2] Heidegger later abandons this priority of *Dasein* as the site for an inquiry into Being itself. In this book, I have focused on the early Heidegger before the turning, or *Kehre*, because of Heidegger's entanglement with profound questions of subjectivity and temporality in conjunction with a powerful engagement with Kant. Although for the later Heidegger, as well as for some postmodern thinkers, subjectivity is seen as a dead end, this study mines the theological implications of powerful philosophical investigations into the self. According to this reading, the self remains a crucial, contested, fragmented, constructed, essential(ized) concept in contemporary discourse. Subjectivity is neither simply identical, nor composed of an identity which subsumes or sublates difference, but an identity riven with differences. These differences or becomings compose a fragile identity, or what Deleuze and Guattari call a "fragmentary whole."[3]

The self as a concept or category is both a site of sinister ideological manipulation as well as an agent of freedom in social and political terms. It is also the site of spiritual transformation, whether marked as such in explicit or implicit terms. In this sense, the self is a crucial term for theological discourse. Due to the processes of subjectivization and formalization described in Chapter One, in some respects the self has replaced God in modernity as a central theological category. This reading of Kant suggests that subjectivity is a more central category and more inherently "theological" than God relative to the dynamics of the First and Third Critiques. I will return to a broader historical-theoretical discussion of subjectivity at the end of the chapter in the context of theology's relationship to anthropology and psychoanalysis.

I have demonstrated an irreducible internal sublimity of the self, which is essentially related to temporality and imagination in Kant. This sublimity of the self is related to certain conceptual figurations of life and death. Thinking is living. That is, humans do more than think, but consciousness accompanies all of one's actions and beliefs. In a broad sense, thinking can include feelings, emotions, willing, etc., as a characterization of the ability to make sense of (react to) experience. To grasp the transcendental conditions for thinking is to isolate the possibility of living in the world and being human, which is an experience common to anyone who can read this book. If thinking broadly considered represents the possibility of life in general, the sublime marks a radical discontinuity or break which could be characterized as death. The sublime represents terrifying excess, loss of control, and in-breaking of imagination beyond the ability of reason and understanding to bring it to order, which is related to Augustine's classical conception of the will.

For Augustine, the fallen will, represented paradigmatically by orgasm, testifies to a loss of control and rationality. The will's inability to bring itself under complete control indicates the presence of a sublime aspect of the will, understood in a negative rather than positive sense. Although I have generalized and universalized what Augustine would call the will in terms of sublime thinking or representation, the prelapsarian will is not an object of possible human experience, and therefore approximates to a Kantian thing-in-itself.[4] In this way, I am making an analogy between an Augustinian will and a Kantian understanding in a way that broadens and generalizes Kant's understanding of pure reason to an existential process of thinking, willing, and living. This death which the sublime attests to, however, makes life itself possible, because it is the very activity of the Schematism which allows knowing to occur, or, analogously, the very failure of the will to exert total control or self-mastery is what allows humans to will at all.

In *Being and Time*, Heidegger defines human *Dasein* as being-unto-death; that is, human beings are aware of their mortality and finitude. In *Aporias*, Derrida shows that while Heidegger wants a resolute orientation to death to result in authenticity, the death that Heidegger describes already affects or infects *Dasein*; thus death is inauthenticating, or disappropriating. "If death," Derrida writes, "the most proper possibility of *Dasein*, is the possibility of its impossibility, death becomes the most improper possibility and the most ex-propriating, the most inauthenticating one."[5] Derrida claims that death is an aporia, or an impassable passage, but as the paradigmatic aporia, the "nonaccess to death as such"—the fact that we are constituted by an experience which we cannot endure as a complete and total experience—means that "the ultimate aporia is the impossibility of the aporia *as such*."[6] There is no absolute cutting off of life from death: "circumscription is the impossible," and dying means awaiting one another —awaiting oneself, awaiting the other, and awaiting oneself as another in a relation of mourning, because we are always already dying.[7]

Derrida's logic of aporia applies to the sublime, understood as an ecstatic event which marks thinking as living and makes it possible, even as it marks it as finite, that is, in relation to death as its end. The sublime moment of thinking, understood as a breakdown of thinking when it attempts to think itself thinking, when it attempts to think (aesthetically, subjectively) an infinite series in one (re)presentation, understood as the source and ground of thinking and being, inserts itself between what we call life and death (which cannot be thought as simple opposites), distributing both as effects of experience.

The Schematism represents the process of coming-to-representation, but this process is marked by a fissure, wound, or aporia which prevents us from becoming fully conscious of what it allows us to become conscious of. The sublime refers to a violence or dizziness which thinking undergoes in trying to represent anything at all, a schematism unmoored from an objective synthesis. This sublimity refers not simply to an object, but to the process of thinking itself. This sublimity is theological, because it concerns us ultimately; it has to do with being and non-being, because it makes up who we are by constituting human subjectivity. In *The Gathering of Reason*, John Sallis claims that the questions Kant addresses with the ideas of reason—"the question whether the soul is an indivisible unity, whether there is freedom, whether a supreme cause of the world exists—these are questions of ultimate human concern."[8] I am suggesting that in some respects the central epistemological question which concerns knowing and thinking, basically the possibility of making sense out of any experience, is a more fundamental question in the Kantian critique, and is of at least as great a concern.

II

The sublime represents what Lyotard calls a proliferation or excess of form-giving capacity which cannot be captured in a determinate image or form.[9] The sublime aspect of thinking which manifests itself in the Schematism attests to a straining, bending, or breaking of form, because the process of thinking distorts the status of the object which is thought. We could think of reflection in its etymological sense of the action of bending back, or folding upon itself, and consider the sublime moment in thinking as a folding of form.[10] This folding is the reflexivity of attempting to think that which is thinking. This activity, which is what makes thinking itself possible, also marks a disruption or a fissuring which is constitutive of subjectivity.

This folding of form, or a bending back of form upon itself in an attempt to mirror the process of *Einbildungskraft*, provides a way of understanding Tillich's definition of religion as the depth aspect of culture. Instead of inhabiting some interior spatial realm, one could think of religion as the human activity of giving expression to this process of thinking and living, which always exceeds any capacity to represent. Religion cannot be identified with any particular realm of culture, but it exists at the depth of every aspect of culture, that is, at the moment any region of culture or human activity folds back upon itself in its attempt to give representation to itself. This folding of form, of any particular form of culture, testifies to a sublime moment which cannot be fully contained by the determinate form or image it takes. Theology for Tillich is then second-order reflection on religion, or the attempts to grapple with and understand this process, even as it evades all attempts to render it determinate and fully knowable.

In a Kantian sense, religion cannot be understood as an autonomous realm of culture, and thus it does not require or possess a critique. For the most part, Kant appends religion to morality, especially in *Religion Within the Limits of Reason Alone*.[11] After Kant, many intellectuals have over-taken a division of culture into three spheres of cognition/philosophy/science, morality, and art. In addition, many intellectuals concerned with religion have been constrained either to connect religion to one of these realms or to carve out an independent space for it to occupy. Although Schleiermacher tries to carve out a place for religion in the realm of feeling, following the *Critique of Judgment*, Tillich realizes the futility of these attempts to situate religion in relation to science, philosophy or reflective thinking, ethical or moral willing, and artistic or aesthetic feeling. He calls religion "the dimension of depth" in human spiritual life, or each of these three functions of cognition, morality, and aesthetics. Depth for Tillich is a metaphor for "that which is ultimate, infinite, unconditional" in human spiritual life.[12] Religion as ultimate concern manifests itself in each of these three spheres, not on the surface, as they understand themselves in their own terms, but in their depth or at their limits.

In his *Theology of Culture*, Tillich considers the attempts to locate religion in various domains of human spiritual life. He relates the story, ever since Kant's critiques laid the groundwork for intellectual categorization, "of how religion goes from one spiritual function to the other to find a home, and is either rejected or swallowed by them."[13] Religion turns from the moral to the cognitive to the aesthetic function, and then to feeling. Finally,

> religion suddenly realizes that it does not need such a place, that it does not need such a home. It is at home everywhere, namely in the depth of all functions of man's [sic] spiritual life. Religion is the depth dimension in all of them.[14]

Religion does not have a home or a place in any one of the commonly demarcated spheres of human activity, which is why the attempt to locate a determinative space for religion has become impossible. As the depth dimension of any or all of these functions of human living, however, religion represents the limits of each function. As the depth dimension of individual faculties or functions, religion appears as sublime, because one can identify a sphere or phenomenon as religious only when its self-representation breaks down.

For Tillich, the metaphor "depth" drives his theology. It is the depth of reason, not the structure or logos of reason which breaks through to revelation and God as being-itself.[15] Tillich also calls this depth aspect of reason the "abyss," which must be understood in relation to the Kantian sublime, where the struggle between reason and imagination sets up a vibration (*Erschütterung*) which consists in "a rapid alternation of repulsion from, and attraction to, one and the same object." This vibration is caused by the proliferation of forms of an imagination striving for infinity, and it creates "an abyss in which the imagination is afraid to lose itself."[16] The abyssal or depth aspect of reason is more profound than the structure of reason for Tillich, because it is in the depth of reason that the possibility of being and non-being of an object or person resides.

We can also apply this discussion of faculties to the faculties of understanding, imagination, and reason. In each of these cases, religion for Tillich refers to the limit at which point each faculty is surpassed as it is in itself, and points to something beyond it to which it is unable to achieve representation. This limit is a folding of form upon itself, which I have called alternately Schematism and sublime. This folding is also a proliferation or stretching of form, rather than a breakdown or inadequacy. Form itself expands and folds; the object which is being represented undergoes a certain shattering regarding its determinate form.

In *Kant's Critical Philosophy*, Deleuze attempts to define the limits of intellectual and cultural representation by isolating a "higher form" of each faculty. What is specifically important in the reading of Kant by Deleuze, in relation to Tillich, is that where Deleuze in each of the critiques asks whether there is a "higher faculty" of knowledge, desire and feeling, this relates to Tillich's efforts to locate "religion" at the depth of each faculty.[17] Since this higher faculty (Deleuze) relates to the supersensible, it occurs at a structurally similar point where Tillich indicates depth. In both cases, the faculties (as modes of knowing) surpass themselves and attempt to give voice to the unsurpassable itself. For Deleuze, the sublime represents the paradigmatic case of a higher faculty, because it is the discordant accord of reason and imagination which raises the faculties beyond themselves and gives rise to a higher faculty of feeling.[18]

This surpassing of limits by the various faculties in their interrelations is what gives rise to a "higher form" of a faculty of knowledge, desire, and feeling. According to Deleuze by way of Tillich, faculties can be understood both as zones of culture and as modes of knowing. For Deleuze, faculties are both the straightforward Kantian powers of imagination, reason, understanding, etc., as well as broader areas of knowing (philosophy or science), desire (morality), and feeling (aesthetics). These zones of culture, which Tillich calls dimensions of human spiritual life, cannot be understood as spheres of religion except in their depth or their higher form, that is, at the point or moment when they surpass themselves and (attempt to) give representation to the unrepresentable itself, which is the sublime. The sublime, understood as the formlessness of pure form, or the disorientation induced by the dizzying proliferation of forms, introduces disorientation at the limits of cultural understanding and expression, as well as within the limits of human thinking itself. This disorientation provides an important source of religious meaning, and calls for serious theological reflection.

Both the metaphors of depth (Tillich) and height (Deleuze) are in some sense arbitrary, and both attempt to express a similar insight, that is, the activity of the folding of form back upon itself in the attempt to represent what the form is in itself, which is only partially successful. I am suggesting that we follow Tillich and think of religion as the breakdown of these autonomous spheres of culture, not in the sense of the dissolution of such spheres, but in their "depth" or "higher form," that is, where they fold back upon themselves in their attempt to represent the cultural or psychological dynamics that make them possible in the first place. In this sense, theology can be defined as the thinking of this sublime religiosity, that is, the reflection which pursues or traces the folds to their very "breaking-point." The breaking-point occurs when the cultural or theoretical folds bend back upon themselves in an impossible way, which gives rise to anxiety and horror, but at the same time this very folding gives rise to thinking. Theological thinking, then, retraces the folds which make thought possible in the first place, which is an impossible and infinite task, but no less necessary. Religion understood as the sublime, therefore, would exist at (as) the joint or hinge of this form, and theology then is the attempt to reflect theoretically on religion. Theology would then be another fold or folding, but it would be a second-order fold in the way Tillich defines theology as second-order reflection on religion. Theology can be defined as the attempt to grasp the folding of form which is religion, but this is not simply possible, because of the dynamic nature of the activity of the religious (sublime) folding. At the same time, theology itself as second-order folding is also a dynamic and sublime activity.

III

This juxtaposition of Tillich with Deleuze regarding Kant is another way of understanding the dissolution of the sacred in European modernity, as well as the inability simply to relocate it anywhere. As I have indicated in the first chapter, theology is utopian (no-place), in exile, or homeless, but that by no means eliminates its importance understood as the restlessness underlying or inhabiting all of our efforts to live and think and communicate. In post-Kantian terms, religion cannot be completely divorced from theology, understood as an attempt at intellectual sense-making by a religious tradition. After the Kantian "Copernican revolution," we cannot simply identify any object as religious in a phenomenological sense without implicating ourselves and our own processes of knowing. Therefore, the very identification of a phenomenon as religious is a theological act.[19]

Historically, however, European modernity represents a displacement or disjunction of God. God is not an object of experience, in a Kantian framework, and the divine can only be expressed negatively insofar as it relates to and disturbs the process of thinking. God as a regulative idea provides subjective orientation in thinking, and God as negativity in the sublime disrupts or disorients thinking (even as it makes it possible in the first place). For this reason, Kant undertakes a "Critique of all Theology" (A631/B659), just as Winquist calls for a "philosophical theology . . . which is committed to the task of providing a transcendental critique of theology."[20] A transcendental critique of theology is a theological critique of all determinate forms of theological expression, even as it attempts to express or represent that which it cannot represent. A formal theology, a theology concerning the generation of forms, or what Tillich calls the depth dimension of culture, is metonymical, because it attends to substitutions and transformations on a shared plane, rather than metaphorical, that is, dealing with a substitution from a region of transcendence.[21]

One might be tempted to call the sublime as condition of unrepresentability itself God, but this is possible only in a metonymical sense. The limits of human representation are themselves metaphorical (in a broad sense), not literal, and therefore we do not know what we mean when we assign the word God to that which is unrepresentable.[22] According to Robert P. Scharlemann, the word "God," defined by Anselm as "that than which nothing greater can be thought," introduces a negativity into language and signifies in a paradoxical way what the word "word" (or any actual word in language) does not. In this project, Scharlemann follows Tillich's general trajectory, developing a paradoxical reading in which God is not "God."[23] If God is not "God," then what is God? For Scharlemann, there is a sense in which the word "word" (or again, any word in language), represents the being of God when God is not being God.[24] Scharlemann's formulation of the "being of God when God is not being God" introduces a radical negativity into thinking, because no word can itself be "that than which nothing greater can be thought," and each word therefore points beyond itself. At the same time, the pressure of thinking God as "that than which nothing greater can be thought" in words, along with thinking language as the "being of God when God is not being God" produces a tension which pushes language (and conceptuality) almost to the breaking point. The ability of language to generate meanings which it cannot contain also occasions sublime phenomena. Theological exigency demands that this tension be held onto, despite desires to flee to a transcendent extra-linguistic or pre-linguistic realm, or to simply accept language, get comfortable within it, and take it for granted.

To meditate creatively upon the concept of God as sublime and to reinterpret it constructively is fruitful. Theology cannot evade the "Death of God," however. The "Death of God" is not simply a literal slogan; it represents a metaphorical or metonymical displacement. When understood in terms of French poststructuralism, it becomes clear that the word God functions as a sign, and however unique a status it claims, within a chain of signification the term God cannot function as a transcendental signified. Interpreted in any literal sense, a Death of God theology appears incoherent, oxymoronic. On the other hand, if Death of God theology represents a development of American pragmatism which brackets the in-itself existence of God as an ontological entity, one can align such a theological tradition, however underground or minor, with contemporary French theory. The "Death of God" represents a conceptual break, because to understand that the word God is a concept is to free oneself from the burden of arguing for the ontological existence or non-existence of that concept. This is what Kant means in the *Critique of Pure Reason* when he claims that existence or being is not a real predicate (A598/B626).

IV

The "Death of God" designates a certain bracketing of the question of the status of God as an entity, and at the same time it also refers to a historical development of European modernity. I am alluding to a certain transition which shifts theological significance from God to the self as a category. This is not merely a process of secularity to be deplored. We must interrogate the possibilities and problems connected with such a shift, which corresponds to Habermas' transition from philosophies of being to philosophies of consciousness. This book isolates a certain moment in the process of a foregrounding of subjectivity in contrast with divinity in the texts of Kant, but it also complicates it in what some may consider a dissolution of subjectivity.

For Thomas J.J. Altizer, the most famous Death of God theologian, Western history represents a kenotic process of God's self-sacrifice in order to become all in all. In a parallel fashion, at a later point in history, the human self also dissolves in order to become total. Subjectivity dissolves into an anonymous humanity.[25] Although I do not endorse the residual metaphysical Hegelianism which clings to his texts, Altizer identifies a historical/cultural process which possesses a certain amount of credibility. I will describe a similarly broad movement at a general level by relating a trajectory from a classical ontological theology to a theological anthropology to a contemporary psychoanalytic theological understanding which remains largely unacknowledged and implicit.

Feuerbach represents the culmination of the shift in understanding inaugurated by Descartes. Descartes emphasizes the irreducible certainty of the I or *cogito* in his *Meditations on First Philosophy*, and this marks a "subjective turn" which characterizes modernity. Once human consciousness becomes the privileged ground of evidence, meaning, and truth, the subject becomes the basis through which to think God. In order for theology to exist, it must elaborate a theological thinking which presents an objective God or reality in terms accessible to a believing subject. Of course, in this development God becomes more and more inaccessible, and ultimately even the subject becomes incredibly complicated and compromised as a ground for knowing. We have seen this occur paradigmatically in Kant. At the same time, however, religion is essentially defined subjectively in terms of belief or faith.

Feuerbach is the first theologian to draw the obvious conclusion: "the true sense of Theology is Anthropology."[26] Despite the desire of theology to reach God, it becomes more and more entangled in the human subject's modes of knowing, feeling, and belief. In *The Christian Faith*, Schleiermacher, who is considered the first modern theologian, defines religion as a "feeling of absolute dependence," and God as a "Whence" or unknown source of that feeling.[27]

In this historical sense, anthropology becomes the necessary form of theological discourse, because in order to be credible it must treat the status of the believing subject, or what Tillich calls the "reception" of revelation.[28] As theology becomes anthropology, anthropology develops as an autonomous discipline. Anthropology originally represents a general understanding of the human being, which is expressed in Kant's *Anthropology from a Pragmatic Point of View*, as well as in the culmination of Kant's three questions "What can I know? What ought I to do? What may I hope?" in the question "What is man?" (A805/B833). Anthropology in the late nineteenth century transforms itself into a regional investigation of "other" cultures and peoples. The objects of such anthropological inquiry are originally defined as "primitives"—the indigenous cultures subjected to Western scrutiny were studied in order to learn about the origins of human nature in general, although such efforts cannot be separated from Western colonialism and imperialism.

This study of other cultures in a derogatory manner has rebounded self-critically into an affirmative cultural anthropology and a philosophical discourse of the "Other," defined not only as the alterity of a member of another culture but also as the irreducible alterity of oneself. A postmodern theology influenced by Derrida and Emmanuel Levinas celebrates the status of the "other" and at times even exalts God to the status of the ultimate "Other."[29] This fundamental category of alterity confirms the significance of anthropology for contemporary theological discourse. Of course, many traditional theologians, as well as the representatives of Radical Orthodoxy, deplore the subjective turn of modernity and desire that postmodernity represent an abolishing of the subject in order to clear a space for the divine to appear of its own accord. I am suggesting, however, that it is neither credible nor possible to undo such a development (such a fold), and that the only resources honest theologians can petition are ones forged in and through modernity.

I am not opposing the preoccupations with alterity that characterize postmodern philosophical and theological thinking, but this thinking fails at times to acknowledge its dependence on another strand of modern inquiry. At around the same time, and in a different manner from anthropology, Freud inaugurates a psychoanalytic discourse which has permeated popular culture to such an extent that it has assumed the status of a quasi-religious language. Theology has been extremely resistant to psychoanalytic discourse, assuming that psychoanalysis necessarily implies a materialistic reductionism. There are many affinities, however, between a psychoanalytic questioning and my theological reading of the Kantian sublime, which cracks open a certain traditional interpretation of the subject.

In his magisterial study of Freud, *Freud and Philosophy*, Paul Ricoeur conducts an epistemological and ultimately Kantian reading of Freud. Kant introduces a gap between phenomena and noumena that fissures representational thinking. Freud introduces distortion and disguise into that gap in the development of a dream logic or a dreamwork, which attests to unconscious thinking.[30] According to his first topology, an unconscious primary process thinking is distinguished from secondary (preconscious and conscious) processes. Such primary processes can be considered in a Kantian light: as noumenal processes, unconscious thoughts are impossible to discern as phenomenal appearance, and instead must be posited based upon how they distort secondary processes.[31] The secondary processes, then, correspond to the Kantian phenomena which appear and conform to human representation and language. What is especially significant is that Freud embeds both noumenal and phenomenal processes in the depths or heart of the subject.

My reading of the Kantian sublime does not correspond to Freudian sublimation, because sublimation refers to a more Hegelian elevation or sublation of primal drives into aesthetic or artistic pursuits. Sublimation refers to the unsuccessful attempt to sublate libidinal impulses by directing them into social and artistic efforts, which transmute their repressive qualities but preserve their essential libidinal charge. What is decisively characteristic of Freudian sublimation is that it does not work in any total sense; there is always a return of the repressed. The fact that Freud was well-disposed to art but remained critical of religion alters nothing concerning the essential and ultimate failure of sublimation as anything other than a strategy for coping with the power of the drives. Sublimation can be considered a failure insofar as it is understood to elevate the subject or ego to a higher plane above the region of the libido and the drives. As discussed in Chapter Five, "subl(im)ation" is the function Kant appeals to in the dynamical sublime, where the human mind reflects on its ability to transcend raging nature. This elevation is also what underlies Hegel's notion of *Aufhebung*, which he derives from the Third Critique. To appeal to sublimation to raise an individual or group above a material onto a spiritual plane is disallowed by Freud consistently. On the other hand, sublimation can be thought of as a redirection or substitution of libidinal drives, which alters their interrelations and brings about a new arrangement of life, conceived on the same plane.[32] Actually, what Freud calls sublimation can be better understood along the lines of Kantian beauty, which consists in a free play of imagination and understanding in a purposiveness without purpose or a finality without end.

In his essay on "The Uncanny," on the other hand, Freud identifies the real source of the Kantian sublime, as the estrangement of the ego from itself at its most basic and familiar level. The uncanny perception or feeling produces a negative pleasure, just like the Kantian sublime. The purposiveness refers to a felt sense of familiarity, almost a *déja vu*, while the negativity inherent in the feeling attests to the radical disorientation it introduces, because such a feeling cannot quite be possessed or owned. Furthermore, Freud comes to identify the source of this negativity with death. Freud explicitly identifies the source of the uncanny judgment with the compulsion to repeat which constitutes the death drive when he writes that "whatever reminds us of this inner 'compulsion to repeat' is perceived as uncanny."[33] The Kantian sublime thus passes into the Freudian unconscious, and reappears, most explicitly and powerfully, in the death drive.

In *Beyond the Pleasure Principle*, Freud tentatively introduces the hypothesis of the death drive, which resists the life drives of the pleasure principle in order to return to a state of inorganic stasis. In this sense, Freud comes to the terrifying realization that "the aim of all life is death."[34] The sublime is the death drive which is experienced as an uncanny disruption of subjectivity at its very core, and any authentic theological thinking must grapple with the profound logic of this death drive, as well as the difficulties surrounding sublimation. At the same time, however, this very death drive perpetuates life, according to Freud, because "the organism wishes to die in its own fashion."[35] The death drive represents a detour on the path towards death because the living being resists any external circumstances "which might help it attain its life's aim rapidly—by a kind of short-circuit."[36] The division which constitutes the germ cells or life drives does not simply oppose the death drive; rather it manifests an extraordinary occasion of the death drive. The organism struggles to divide, to reproduce itself, aiming at its death, which is the goal or purpose, and yet the tension of this reproduction is productive of further life. Here life and death are intimately related, and Freud's extreme speculation represents a powerful example of the Kantian sublime.

In crucial respects, Freud's most speculative work remains a myth, even as he draws upon the myth of Aristophanes to fashion his interpretation. Such a mythical status, however, does not belie the profound importance of his thinking, or the challenge for contemporary theological thinking to take it up. Freudian psychoanalysis moves within a broadly Kantian framework, even as it breaches many of Kant's conclusions, and offers a fruitful arena for further theological reflection. Carl A. Raschke has asserted Freud's significance for a postmodern theology of the body, when stating that Freudian psychoanalysis "has shifted the grounds of discourse itself" from a Kantian analytic towards a "transcendental somatics."[37] Freud embeds truth within the body of the subject, which is intimately interior and at the same time radically foreign to conscious representational understanding. For Raschke, the logic of the Freudian "double sentence," which erases as it writes, inaugurates a postmodern ontology of the body erotic, in which the text of the unconscious "discloses the body that has not yet been inscribed" in an eschatological manner.[38]

For both Freud and Raschke, the body is not a simple immediate given, but it expresses a complex multiple signification, and its strategies of deception, distortion, and disguise undermine a clear logic of straightforward theological phenomenology. Psychoanalytic theory at its most powerful represents a persistent implication with, and insistent interrogation of, the sublime, which radically distorts thinking even as it engenders it.

Conclusion

This reading of the Kantian sublime figures the negative imagination as desire, which provides important resources for postmodern thinking. Although the sublime is thought in Kant and in this book as a development of subjectivity, it represents a fissuring of subjectivity in what can be viewed as a historical development characteristic of modernity. Therefore, to the extent that one can locate the sublime, it takes a position anterior to the subject, that is, just before or beyond it. And since the sublime represents what we can know now as God, one can draw the further consequence, along with Lacan, that God is (the) unconscious.[39] In fact, one can claim that in his notion of the sublime, Kant "discovers" what later becomes known as the Freudian unconscious.

The logic of the unconscious is in important ways posited rather than clearly understood, and its effects are felt in a disorienting "anaesthesis" (Lyotard) which is the source of religious meaning today. Kant perceives this central insight, that it is the discord of human powers that disrupt human understanding and subjectivity, and give rise to the sublime, even though he strongly resists these conclusions. The contemporary crisis of representation is a crisis of intelligibility, and despite calls to return to premodern notions which were supposedly previously intelligible, or theological aesthetic sensibilities which revolt at any "tarrying with the negative," any honest theological thinking must attend to that very dis-orientation.[40] Although claims of unintelligibility are characterized as dogmatic by dogmatic believers, such problems with intelligibility actually provide the possibility for humility, if the calling into question of estab-lished notions of intelligibility by empirical events and experiences allows the space to re-envision intelligibility itself. A sublime intelligibility would be thought as uncanny, and unconscious strategies (which do not simply return to the stage of primary process thinking, but allow the experience of the fracturation of secondary processes to stimulate an elaboration of what might be considered tertiary processes) would be needed to grapple with the distorted logic of aesthetic sensibility which marks the sublime.[41]

In many ways, this reading of Kant pursues the most negative of nega-tive theologies in an apocalyptic way which is relevant for the situation of our contemporary world.[42] A negative theology grapples with ultimate questions but does not simply accept answers uncritically. Broadly under-stood, such a negative theology exhibits a restlessness or discontent regard-ing the immediate world; it troubles experience in such a way that theology does not conceive itself as a result but rather a process of questioning or interrogating existence in a meaningful thinking. A theology of the sub-lime, which is unable to be harnessed by reason toward moral ends, also resonates with a felt sense of disorientation, dizzying change, and the perceived breakdown of both social structures and patterns of thought. Of course, this deterritorialization may be the condition for a new reterritorialization,[43] a new world order, a global village, or a universal economic market, whether conceived in utopian or dystopian terms.[44] This theology of the sublime, however, situates itself in the interstice between a dissolution of all established orders of thinking and any new, reconstructive thinking, whether understood as an absolute *novum* or a return to a pure past.

Notes

Introduction

1 For Kant's place in the context of German philosophy, see Lewis White Beck, *Early German Philosophy: Kant and His Predecessors* (Cambridge, Mass.: Harvard University Press, 1969).

2 Immanuel Kant, *Critique of Pure Reason*, translated by Norman Kemp Smith (New York: St. Martin's Press, 1965), Preface to the Second Edition, p. 22. In the future, I have followed the standard convention of referring to the A (1781) or B (1787) edition and the page number(s) of the original German edition in the text. Thus, for this reference, Bxvi.

3 The two major commentaries on Kant's *Critique of Pure Reason* written in English are Norman Kemp Smith, *A Commentary on Kant's "Critique of Pure Reason"* (New York: Humanities Press, 1962), and H.J. Paton, *Kant's Metaphysics of Experience*, two volumes (London: George Allen & Unwin Ltd., 1951). See also, A.C. Ewing, *A Short Commentary on Kant's "Critique of Pure Reason"* (Chicago: University of Chicago Press, 1967).

4 See P.F. Strawson, *The Bounds of Sense: An Essay on Kant's "Critique of Pure Reason"* (London: Methuen & Co. Ltd., 1966); Jonathan Bennett, *Kant's Analytic* (Cambridge: Cambridge University Press, 1966); Paul Guyer, *Kant and the Claims of Knowledge* (Cambridge: Cambridge University Press, 1987); and Henry E. Allison, *Kant's Transcendental Idealism: An Interpretation and Defense* (New Haven: Yale University Press, 1983). For my strategy of reading Kant, I found Allison the most useful, even if too unquestioningly apologetic for nearly all of Kant's major arguments.

5 *alles-zermalmende*—see John H. Zammito, *The Genesis of Kant's "Critique of Judgment"* (Chicago: University of Chicago Press, 1992), p. 232.

6 Quoted in Peter D. Fenves, *A Peculiar Fate: Metaphysics and World-History in Kant* (Ithaca: Cornell University Press, 1991), p. 3. Fenves goes on to say that, "Only one of these slogans ever constituted a movement, but the two belong together."

7 The German word *Einbildungskraft* refers to the productive power of imagination, which mediates the synthesis of the manifold of sensory intuitions to the unity of conceptual understanding, rather than the reproductive power of imagination, or the imaging of an intuition.

8 Paul Tillich, *Systematic Theology*, Vol. One (Chicago: University of Chicago Press, 1951), p. 37.

9 Friedrich Nietzsche, *Ecce Homo*, translated by R.J. Hollingdale (London: Penguin Books, 1979), p. 68. See also the excellent study by Tyler T. Roberts, *Contesting Spirit: Nietzsche, Affirmation, Religion* (Princeton: Princeton University Press, 1998).

1 Kantian critical philosophy as theology

1 For a distinction between coarse- and fine-grained description, see Murray Gell-Mann, *The Quark and the Jaguar: Adventures in the Simple and the Complex* (New York: W.H. Freeman and Co., 1994).

2 *Theology at the End of the Century: A Dialogue on the Postmodern with Thomas J.J. Altizer, Mark C. Taylor, Charles E. Winquist and Robert P. Scharlemann*, edited by Robert P. Scharlemann (Charlottesville: University Press of Virginia, 1990), p. 1.

3 Ibid., p. 2.

4 Mark C. Taylor, *Erring: A Postmodern A/theology* (Chicago: University of Chicago Press, 1984), p. 48.

5 Gianni Vattimo, *The End of Modernity*, translated by Jon R. Snyder (Baltimore: Johns Hopkins University Press, 1988), p. 166.

6 See Martin Heidegger, *Being and Time*, translated by John Macquarrie and Edward Robinson (New York: Harper & Row, 1962), p. 157: "for as 'care' the Being of Dasein in general is to be defined."

7 Michel Foucault, *The Order of Things: An Archaeology of the Human Sciences* (New York: Vintage Books, 1973).

8 See Charles Taylor, *Sources of the Self: The Making of Modern Identity* (Cambridge, MA: Harvard University Press, 1989), and Seyla Benhabib, *Situating the Self: Gender, Community and Postmodernism in Contemporary Ethics* (New York: Routledge, 1992).

9 *The Modern Subject: Conceptions of the Self in Classical German Philosophy*, edited by Karl Ameriks and Dieter Sturma (Albany: State University of New York Press, 1995), p. 1.

10 Tillich, *Systematic Theology*, Vol. One, p. 12.

11 Ibid., p. 12.

12 Ibid., p. 12.

13 Paul Tillich, *Theology of Culture* (London: Oxford University Press, 1959), p. 7.

14 Tillich, *Systematic Theology*, Vol. One, p. 12.

15 Paul Tillich, *Dynamics of Faith* (New York: Harper & Row, 1957), p. 44.

16 Tillich, *Systematic Theology*, Vol. One, p. 43.

17 Charles E. Winquist, *Desiring Theology* (Chicago: University of Chicago Press, 1995), p. 64.

18 In a footnote added to the B edition (B519), Kant claims that his doctrine of transcendental idealism can also be titled "formal idealism, to distinguish it from material idealism, that is, to distinguish it from the usual type of idealism which doubts or denies the existence of outer things themselves."

19 Tillich, *Theology of Culture*, p. 137.

20 Ibid., p. 137.

21 See Jürgen Habermas, *Postmetaphysical Thinking: Philosophical Essays*, translated by William Mark Hohengarten (Cambridge MA: MIT Press, 1992), p. 12.

22 Immanuel Kant, *Critique of Practical Reason*, translated by Lewis White Beck (New Jersey: Prentice-Hall, 1993), p. 26.

23 See David Hume, *An Inquiry Concerning Human Understanding* (Buffalo: Prometheus Books, 1988), pp. 55–74.

24 Immanuel Kant, *Prolegomena to any Future Metaphysics*, translated by Lewis White Beck (Indianapolis: Bobbs-Merrill Company, Inc., 1950), p. 66.

25 Valla proved that the Donation of Constantine, upon which Rome based its historical claim to primacy, was a forgery, and Erasmus, using Valla's *Annotationes*, or textual criticism of the Latin Vulgate Bible, was spurred to make a new translation of the New Testament from the original Greek. See

Johann Huizinga, *Erasmus and the Age of Reformation* (New York: Harper & Row, 1957), p. 90.

26 See Martin Luther, "The Freedom of a Christian," translated by W.A. Lambert, in *Martin Luther: Three Treatises* (Philadelphia: Fortress Press, 1970).

27 See *Lessing's Theological Writings*, translated by Henry Chadwick (Stanford: Stanford University Press, 1957), pp. 9–29.

28 See the contemporary work of the Jesus Seminar, and also J.D. Crossan, *The Historical Jesus: the Life of a Jewish Mediterannean Peasant* (San Francisco: HarperCollins, 1991).

29 Calvin reads a Platonic immortality of the soul into the Old Testament in his *Institutes of the Christian Religion*, edited by John T. McNeill and translated by Ford Lewis Battles (Philadelphia: Westminster Press, 1960), Vol. I, p. 434. On Calvin's Renaissance Humanism, see William J. Bouwsma, *John Calvin: A Sixteenth Century Portrait* (New York: Oxford University Press, 1988). Many Protestant theologians are anxious to separate the Renaissance and the Reformation, for polemical purposes, but Calvin was raised in an environment of French Christian Humanism, personified by the figure of Jacques Léfevre d'Etaples, from which he never completely dissociated himself.

30 Charles H. Long, *Significations: Signs, Symbols and Images in the Interpretation of Religion* (Philadelphia: Fortress Press, 1986), p. 7.

31 Immanuel Kant, "What is Orientation in Thinking?" in *Kant: Political Writings*, edited by Hans Reiss and translated by H.B. Nisbet (Cambridge: Cambridge University Press, 1991), p. 237.

32 Ibid., p. 240.

33 Ibid., pp. 240–1.

34 Ibid., p. 239.

35 Ibid., p. 239.

36 Gianni Vattimo, *The Transparent Society*, translated by David Webb (Baltimore: Johns Hopkins University Press, 1992), p. 47.

37 Ibid., p. 51.

38 Ibid., p. 69.

39 Jean-François Lyotard brings together Benjamin's aesthetics of shock and the Kantian sublime in what Lyotard calls an "anesthetics" in *Heidegger and "the jews,"* translated by Andreas Michel and Mark S. Roberts (Minneapolis: University of Minnesota Press, 1990), p. 31.

40 For a more explicit discussion of the Kantian sublime as the religious, see Clayton Crockett, "On the Disorientation of the Study of Religion," in *What is Religion? Origins, Definitions & Explanations*, edited by Thomas A. Idinopulos and Brian C. Wilson (Leiden: Brill, 1998).

41 See Rudolf Otto, *The Idea of the Holy*, translated by John W. Harvey (New York: Oxford University Press, 1950).

42 Vattimo, *The End of Modernity*, p. 172.

43 Ibid., pp. 172–3.

44 Ibid., p. 179.

45 The Latin word *radix* means "root."

46 Vattimo writes, referring to Max Weber: "This may appear to be a very abstract generalization, but it is no longer so if we translate *Verwindung* into a term which is much more familiar to historians of Western civilization, namely the term 'secularization.'" *The End of Modernity*, p. 179.

47 See Gabriel Vahanian, *God and Utopia* (New York: The Seabury Press, 1977), pp. 112–13.

48 Vahanian, *God and Utopia*, p. 19. See also *L'utopie chrétienne* (Paris: Desclée de Brouwer, 1992).

49 *God and Utopia*, p. 116.

50 Gilles Deleuze, *Bergsonism*, translated by Hugh Tomlinson and Barbara Habberjam (New York: Zone Books, 1991), p. 15.
51 Ibid., p. 15.

2 On modern sublimity: the challenge of Radical Orthodoxy

1 In addition to the works of Milbank discussed below, see the collections of essays, *Post-Secular Philosophy: Between Philosophy and Theology*, edited by Phillip Blond (London: Routledge, 1998) and *Radical Orthodoxy: A New Theology*, edited by John Milbank, Catherine Pickstock and Graham Ward (London: Routledge, 1999). A more cautious and moderate expression can be found in Graham Ward's solid comparison, *Barth, Derrida and the Language of Theology* (Cambridge: Cambridge University Press, 1995). On the other hand, Catherine Pickstock's book, *After Writing: On the Liturgical Consummation of Philosophy* (Oxford: Blackwell, 1998), represents a rhetorically plausible but critically suspect reading of Plato and Derrida, the latter of whom is dubbed a "necrophiliac."
2 Alasdair MacIntyre, *After Virtue: A Study in Moral Theory*, 2nd ed. (Notre Dame: University of Notre Dame Press, 1997).
3 Alasdair MacIntyre, *Three Rival Versions of Moral Enquiry: Encyclopedia, Genealogy and Tradition* (Notre Dame: University of Notre Dame Press, 1990), p. 137.
4 Ibid., p. 140.
5 John Milbank, *Theology and Social Theory: Beyond Secular Reason* (Oxford: Blackwell, 1990), p. 5.
6 Ibid., pp. 4–5.
7 On this question, see Max Horkheimer and Theodor W. Adorno, *Dialectic of Enlightenment*, translated by John Cumming (New York: Continuum, 1993).
8 Douglas Hedley, "Should Divinity Overcome Metaphysics? Reflections on John Milbank's Theology Beyond Secular Reason and Confessions of a Cambridge Platonist," *Journal of Religion* 80: 2, April 2000, p. 280.
9 See Stephen Toulmin, *Cosmopolis: The Hidden Agenda of Modernity* (Chicago: University of Chicago Press, 1992).
10 For a good contextual discussion of these historical issues in early Christianity, see Robert Wilken, *The Christians as the Romans Saw Them* (New Haven: Yale University Press, 1986).
11 On the distinction between anti-Judaism and anti-semitism, especially as it applies to the theology of Karl Barth, see Katherine Sondregger, *That Jesus Christ was Born a Jew: Karl Barth's "Doctrine of Israel"* (University Park: Pennsylvania State University Press, 1992).
12 See Peter Canning's dense and powerful discussion in "Jesus Christ Holocaust: Fabulation of the Jews in Christian and Nazi History," *Journal for Cultural and Religious Theory* 1: 2, April 2000, *www.jcrt.org*.
13 *Martin Luther: Selections from his Writings*, edited by John Dillenberger (New York: Doubleday, 1962), p. 117.
14 John Milbank, *The Word Made Strange: Theology, Language, Culture* (Cambridge, Mass.: Blackwell, 1997), pp. 10–11.
15 Rodolphe Gasché, *The Tain of the Mirror: Derrida and the Philosophy of Reflection* (Cambridge, Mass.: Harvard University Press, 1986), p. 274.
16 Milbank, *The Word Made Strange*, p. 12.
17 See Milbank, *The Word Made Strange*, Chapter Three, "Pleonasm, Speech and Writing," pp. 55–83.
18 Ibid., p. 1.
19 Ibid., p. 10.

20 Phillip Blond, Introduction to *Post-Secular Philosophy*, p. 15.
21 Ibid., p. 15.
22 Jean-Luc Marion, "God and Ontotheology," translated by Bettina Bergo, in *Post-Secular Philosophy*, p. 82.
23 See Blond's emphasis in the Introduction to *Post-Secular Philosophy* on "the possibility of a higher phenomenology" which excludes any possibility of a psychoanalytic theology (p. 24). For Blond, because meaning is posited beyond or below the surface appearance or phenomena, psychoanalysis stands within the lineage of a (sublime) Kantian noumenality and is an "essentially a-theistic discourse" (p. 45). On the other hand, according to Blond, "God is and must be thought to be entirely phenomenal" (p. 49).
24 Hans Urs von Balthasar, *The Glory of the Lord: A Theological Aesthetics,* Vol. II: *Studies in Theological Style: Clerical Styles*, translated by Andrew Louth, Francis McDonagh and Brian McNeil (Edinburgh: T. & T. Clark, 1984), p. 11.
25 Ibid., p. 11.
26 Ibid., p. 12.
27 Ibid., p. 12.
28 Milbank, *Theology and Social Theory*, p. 307.
29 Ibid., p. 427.
30 Ibid., p. 427.
31 Ibid., p. 376.
32 Gilles Deleuze and Félix Guattari, *What is Philosophy?* translated by Hugh Tomlinson and Graham Burchell (New York: Columbia University Press, 1994), p. 201.
33 Hedley, "Should Divinity Overcome Metaphysics?" p. 274.
34 See *The Other Heading, Reflections on Today's Europe*, translated by Pascale-Anne Brault and Michael B. Naas (Bloomington: Indiana University Press, 1992), where Derrida appeals to a Kantian critical tradition at the same time as he reserves the right of deconstruction to be critical (or metacritical) of such straightforward critique. What is especially interesting is his formulation in the Kantian language of *duty*: "The *same duty* dictates cultivating the virtue of such *critique, of the critical idea, the critical tradition*, but also submitting it, beyond critique and questioning, to a deconstructive genealogy that thinks and exceeds it without yet compromising it" (p. 77).
35 Milbank, *The Word Made Strange*, p. 49.
36 See Jean-Luc Marion, *God Without Being: Hors-Texte*, translated by Thomas A. Carlson (Chicago: University of Chicago Press, 1991); Jacques Derrida, *Of Grammatology*, translated by Gayatri Chakravorty Spivak (Baltimore: Johns Hopkins University Press, 1976), p. 158.
37 See *The Word Made Strange*, pp. 84–120, quote p. 118, note 67.
38 See Jean-Luc Marion, *Reduction and Givenness: Investigations of Husserl, Heidegger, and Phenomenology*, translated by Thomas A. Carlson (Evanston: Northwestern University Press, 1998). The main difference in form between Milbank and Marion is that for Milbank philosophy becomes sublated by theology in his work everywhere and at once; there is no possibility for an autonomous philosophy. Marion, on the other hand, elaborates his philosophical studies separately from his theological works, and intends his philosophical investigations to stand on their own, apart from his theological conclusions.
39 Karl Barth, *The Word of God and the Word of Man*, translated by Douglas Horton (Gloucester, Mass.: Peter Smith, 1978), p. 186.
40 Human "symbols of ultimate concern must be expressed symbolically!" or else they become idolatrous. See Tillich, *Dynamics of Faith*, p. 44.
41 Paul Tillich, *Biblical Religion and the Search for Ultimate Reality* (Chicago: University of Chicago Press, 1955), p. 5.

42 Ibid., p. 7.
43 See Talal Asad, *Genealogies of Religion* (Baltimore: Johns Hopkins University Press, 1993).

3 Ontology and linguistics: Heidegger and Lyotard

1 *Being and Time* was published in German in 1927, *Kant and the Problem of Metaphysics* in 1929. *The Differend* was published in French in 1983, while *Lessons on the Analytic of the Sublime* was published in 1991.
2 Martin Heidegger, *Being and Time*, translated by John Macquarrie and Edward Robinson (New York: Harper & Row, 1962), pp. 155, 161.
3 Ibid., p. 370.
4 Kant writes that in a transcendental illusion, we "take the subjective necessity of a connection of our concepts, which is to the advantage of the understanding, for an objective necessity in the determination of things in themselves. This is an illusion . . ." which we cannot prevent but can avoid being deceived by, a "natural and unavoidable dialectic of pure reason" (A297–8/B353–4).
5 Charles M. Sherover, *Heidegger, Kant, and Time* (Bloomington: Indiana University Press, 1971), pp. 28–9.
6 Ibid., p. 21.
7 Martin Heidegger, *Kant and the Problem of Metaphysics*, translated by Richard Taft (Bloomington: Indiana University Press, 1990), p. 1. See also the recently translated 1927–8 lectures, *Phenomenological Interpretation of Kant's "Critique of Pure Reason,"* translated by Parvis Emad and Kenneth Maly (Bloomington: Indiana University Press, 1997), which lays the ground for the interpretation presented in *Kant and the Problem of Metaphysics*. Although significant in terms of the development of Heidegger's philosophy, these lectures do not differ in any decisive way from the conclusions of the book, to which I restrict my study.
8 In an essay on the Transcendental Deduction, Wolfgang Carl writes that "the deduction is one of the most difficult parts of the *Critique*. Modern commentators have referred to it as 'the mystery' or as 'the jungle.'" "Kant's First Drafts of the Deduction of the Categories," in *Kant's Transcendental Deductions: The Three Critiques and the Opus Postumum*, edited by Eckart Förster (Stanford: Stanford University Press, 1989), p. 3.
9 Paton, *Kant's Metaphysic of Experience*, Vol. I, p. 354. In the *Critique of Pure Reason*, A97, Kant replaces this threefold synthesis of knowledge with a twofold synthesis in the second edition, B151.
10 Heidegger, *Kant and the Problem of Metaphysics*, p. 54.
11 Ibid., p. 94.
12 Ibid., p. 95.
13 Ibid., p. 110.
14 Ibid., p. 69. See also Sherover, *Heidegger, Kant and Time*, who writes: "The chapter 'The Schematism' has also been generally regarded as obscure and as 'having been the stumbling block of Kantian interpreters . . . Despite complaints about obscurity, Heidegger regards it as the most carefully written and organized section of the Critique" (p. 102).
15 Heidegger, *Kant and the Problem of Metaphysics*, p. 71.
16 Ibid., p. 123.
17 Frank Schalow, *The Renewal of the Heidegger–Kant Dialogue: Action, Thought and Responsibility* (Albany: State University of New York Press, 1992), p. 45.
18 Ibid., p. 25.
19 Sherover, *Heidegger, Kant, and Time*, p. 222.
20 Heidegger, *Kant and the Problem of Metaphysics*, p. 129.

21 Ibid., p. 131. "Time and the 'I think' no longer stand incompatibly and incomparably at odds, they are the same." See also Sherover, *Heidegger, Kant, and Time*, p. 208.

22 Schalow, *The Renewal of the Heidegger–Kant Dialogue*, p. 196.

23 John Sallis, *Spacings—Of Reason and Imagination in Texts of Kant, Fichte, Hegel* (Chicago: University of Chicago Press, 1987), p. 79.

24 Ibid., p. 79.

25 Although his language of the positive nature of the pure productive power of imagination as the common root of two stems and its possibility for finite transcendence is here criticized as problematic, Heidegger's language and metaphorics of abyss demonstrate a willingness to confront the disturbing aspects of imagination in Kant.

26 Ibid., pp. 79–81.

27 On the notion of triangulation, see Winquist, *Desiring Theology*, p. 57. In a "metonymical strategy for a dialectical triangulation ... two discursive practices [or here, Kantian faculties, can] be brought into intimate proximity with each other, forcing metonymical contiguity and thus be able to pressure each other."

28 Heidegger, *Kant and the Problem of Metaphysics*, p. 110.

29 Schalow, *The Renewal of the Heidegger–Kant Dialogue*, p. 120.

30 See Martin Heidegger, "Kant's Doctrine of the Beautiful," in *Nietzsche*, Vols One and Two, translated by David Farrell Krell (San Francisco: HarperCollins, 1991), pp. 107–14.

31 For an understanding of the importance of Kantian ethics for his political philosophy, see Jean-François Lyotard and Jean Thebault, *Just Gaming*, translated by Wlad Godzich and Brian Massumi (Minneapolis: University of Minnesota Press, 1985).

32 Jean François Lyotard, *The Differend: Phrases in Dispute*, translated by Georges Van Den Abeele (Minneapolis: University of Minnesota Press, 1988), p. xiii.

33 Ibid., p. xi.

34 *Vermögen*. Although usually translated as "faculties," Werner Pluhar, in his translation of the *Critique of Judgment*, renders this term as "powers."

35 See Jonathan Bennett, *Kant's Analytic*, p. 7, for an example of Bennett's rhetoric. "This mistake [it matters little which one, as Kant makes so many 'mistakes'] though unimportant in itself, is a symptom of a major and very insidious defect in Kant's account of the analytic/synthetic distinction, namely the psychological terms in which he states it."

36 Lyotard, *The Differend*, p. 27.

37 Gilles Deleuze, *Kant's Critical Philosophy*, translated by Hugh Tomlinson and Barbara Habberjam (Minneapolis: University of Minnesota Press, 1984), p. 10.

38 Lyotard, *The Differend*, p. 136.

39 Ibid., p. 123.

40 Immanuel Kant, *Critique of Judgment*, translated by Werner Pluhar (Indianapolis: Hackett Publishing Company, 1987), pp. 14–15.

41 Lyotard, Jean-François, *Lessons on the Analytic of the Sublime*, translated by Elizabeth Rottenberg (Stanford: Stanford University Press, 1994), p. 8.

42 See ibid., pp. 8–16.

43 See ibid., pp. 26–32.

44 Kant, *Critique of Judgment*, p. 44.

45 Ibid., p. 54.

46 Deleuze, *Kant's Critical Philosophy*, p. xi.

47 See ibid., pp. 3–4 and passim.

48 Lyotard quotes Kant as follows: "For just as ... in the estimate of the beautiful imagination and *understanding* by their concert ... generate subjective finality

of the mental faculties, so ... imagination and *reason* do so here by their conflict [differend]" (*Lessons*, p. 125).

49 See Hannah Arendt, *Eichmann in Jerusalem: A Report on the Banality of Evil* (New York: Viking Press, 1963).
50 Lyotard, *Lessons*, p. 75.
51 Kant, *Critique of Judgment*, p. 106.
52 Lyotard, *Lessons*, p. 109.
53 Kant, *Critique of Judgment*, p. 106.
54 Ibid., p. 115.
55 Lyotard, *Lessons*, p. 138.
56 Kant, *Critique of Judgment*, p. 106.
57 Lyotard, *Heidegger and "the jews,"* pp. 31–2, 44–5.

4 Temporality, subjectivity and imagination: Kant *avec* Deleuze

1 It is helpful to keep in mind that these "faculties" of imagination and understanding, along with sensory intuition and reason, are all, following Lyotard, heuristic categories which represent linguistic processes of thinking and living, specifically regarding the formation of representations.
2 See Henry E. Allison's defense of this project, *Kant's Transcendental Idealism: An Interpretation and Defense*, p. 8 and passim.
3 Quoted in *Kant: Philosophical Correspondence 1759–99*, edited and translated by Arnulf Zweig (Chicago: University of Chicago Press, 1967), p. 252.
4 On the importance of community for Kant's work as a whole, see Susan Meld Shell, *The Embodiment of Reason: Kant on Spirit, Generation, and Community* (Chicago: University of Chicago Press, 1996). Shell emphasizes community in the Analogies of Experience as a "category of relation," but she does not address community in terms of time and space, and her treatment of the *Critique of Pure Reason* is extremely brief compared to the rest of her admittedly impressive book, see pp. 133–46. Shell also addresses Kant's treatment of imagination and the sublime in his early, pre-critical work, which is a valuable and important study but beyond the scope of this book.
5 See Henri Bergson, *The Creative Mind*, translated by Mabelle L. Andison (New York: Philosophical Library, 1946), p. 11.
6 On the specific use of the term deduction, which does not represent a logical deduction as commonly understood in English, see Dieter Henrich, "Kant's Notion of a Deduction and the Methodological Background of the First *Critique*," in Förster, *Kant's Transcendental Deductions*, pp. 30–46.
7 In the ensuing explication, I am following the second or B edition of the Transcendental Deduction. After demonstrating the significance of subjectivity and its connection with temporality, I will explain the crucial difference between the A and B deductions.
8 Ewing, *A Short Commentary on Kant's "Critique of Pure Reason,"* p. 81.
9 Strawson, *The Bounds of Sense*, p. 162. Henry E. Allison also argues that the Paralogisms of Pure Reason represent Kant's critique of Descartes as well as anyone else who attempts to identify "this formal or transcendental I with the real, or noumenal, self" (*Kant's Transcendental Idealism*, p. 282).
10 See Dieter Henrich, *Identität und Objektivität: Eine Untersuchung über Kants transzendentale Deduktion* (Heidelberg: Carl Winter Universitätsverlag, 1976).
11 Dieter Henrich, "The Proof-Structure of Kant's Transcendental Deduction," *Review of Metaphysics* 22: 4, 1969, pp. 640–59 (quotes pp. 645, 657).
12 Guyer, *Kant and the Claims of Knowledge*, p. 161.
13 Guyer supports a modified version of the so-called "Patchwork Theory," which goes back to Hans Vaihinger and Norman Kemp Smith, who hold that the

Critique of Pure Reason represents different strata written at different times which are then patched together to form a heterogeneous whole. This theory has been attacked as ridiculous and impossible to establish by Lewis White Beck and in a less polemical way by Henry E. Allison. Guyer believes that the Transcendental Deduction was written earlier than the rest of the parts of the First Critique which represent the time-determination theory Guyer supports. In addition, Guyer claims that the chapter on the Schematism was inserted into the First Critique at a relatively late date, and Kant could find no way to satisfactorily incorporate it within the Transcendental Deduction (*Kant and the Claims of Knowledge*, pp. 159–60). I am not interested in the historical composition of the *Critique of Pure Reason* as such, although I do treat it as a heterogeneous text, subject to discrepancies, omissions, strains, and disjunctions. For the purposes of this study, the text of the *Critique of Pure Reason* is treated as a text, that is, a given document rather than an assemblage of diverse sections which are then genealogically traced back to particular periods of Kant's life and work. The Kantian text, however, is not treated as a seamless, homogenous, or (in the worst case) an architectonic whole which functions as a system which cannot be interrogated or analyzed into components.

14 Ernst Cassirer affirms "the unity of time . . . in and through which alone there is for us a unity of consciousness" in the Kantian text. *Kant's Life and Thought*, translated by James Haden (New Haven: Yale University Press, 1981), p. 198.
15 Heidegger, *Kant and the Problem of Metaphysics*, p. 131.
16 Willi Goetschel, *Constituting Critique: Kant's Writing as Critical Praxis*, translated by Eric Schwab (Durham: Duke University Press, 1994), p. 130.
17 Heidegger, *Kant and the Problem of Metaphysics*, pp. 122–9.
18 Ibid., p. 128.
19 Deleuze, *Kant's Critical Philosophy*, p. vii.
20 Ibid., p. vii.
21 Ibid., p. viii.
22 Ibid., p. viii.
23 Ibid., p. ix.
24 See J.G. Fichte, *Science of Knowledge*, translated by Peter Heath (New York: Cambridge University Press, 1982), F.W.J. Schelling, *System of Transcendental Idealism*, translated by Peter Heath (Charlottesville: University of Virginia Press, 1978), and G.W.F. Hegel, *Phenomenology of Spirit*, translated by A.V. Miller (Oxford: Oxford University Press, 1977).
25 Gilles Deleuze, *Difference and Repetition*, translated by Paul Patton (New York: Columbia University Press, 1994), p. 86.
26 Ibid., p. 87.
27 Henrich, "The Proof-Structure of Kant's Transcendental Deduction," p. 646.
28 Deleuze, *Kant's Critical Philosophy*, pp. 3–10.
29 Ibid., p. 51. "It can be seen that the imagination–reason accord is not simply assumed: it is genuinely engendered, engendered in the dissension."
30 Ibid., p. 10.
31 Ibid., p. 4.
32 Ibid., p. xii.

5 The Analytic of the Sublime

1 For an attempt to show the place of the Third Critique within an architectonic framework, see Sarah L. Gibbons, *Kant's Theory of Imagination: Bridging Gaps in Judgment and Experience* (Oxford: Clarendon Press, 1994). Gibbons emphasizes what I call the positive power of imagination, and its ability to overcome the gap between intuitions and concepts in an almost Heideggerian

way, despite her background in analytic philosophy. Another attempt to use the Third Critique to "solve" Kant's problem is the focus on the "Critique of Teleological Judgment" as the second half of the Third Critique, which is able to mediate between the realm of sensible nature addressed by the First Critique, and the realm of supersensible morality, addressed by the Second Critique. See Adina Davidovich, *Religion as a Province of Meaning: The Kantian Foundations of Modern Theology* (Minneapolis: Fortress Press, 1993), and Veronique Zanetti, "Teleology and the Freedom of the Self," in Ameriks and Sturma (eds), *The Modern Subject*, pp. 47–64, as well as Gérard Lebrun, *Kant et la mort de la métaphysique: Essai sur la "Critique de la Faculté de Juger"* (Paris: Librairie Armand Colin, 1970). For the attempt to secure an independent realm of art, see Mikel Dufrenne, *In the Presence of the Sensuous: Essays in Aesthetics*, edited by Mark S. Roberts and Dennis Gallagher (Atlantic Highlands, NJ: Humanities Press International, Inc., 1987), Chapter 6, "The Beautiful," pp. 75–84, and Paul Crowther, *The Kantian Sublime: From Morality to Art* (Oxford: Clarendon Press, 1989).

2 Derrida, *Of Grammatology*, pp. 141–64.

3 Ibid., p. 149.

4 See Derrida, *The Other Heading*, pp. 72–3.

5 On the distortion of the First Critique by the Third, specifically in terms of the sublime and the imagination, see Paul de Man, "Phenomenality and Materiality in Kant," in *The Textual Sublime: Deconstruction and its Differences*, edited by Hugh J. Silverman and Gary E. Aylesworth (Albany, State University of New York Press, 1990), and Sallis, *Spacings*.

6 Kant, *Critique of Judgment*, p. 31.

7 Ibid., p. 32.

8 Ibid., p. 84.

9 Jacques Derrida, *The Truth in Painting*, translated by Geoff Bennington and Ian McCleod (Chicago: University of Chicago Press, 1987), p. 89.

10 Kant, *Critique of Judgment*, p. 62.

11 Dieter Henrich, *Aesthetic Judgment and the Moral Image of the World: Studies in Kant* (Stanford: Stanford University Press, 1992), p. 40.

12 Kant, *Critique of Judgment*, p. 93.

13 See Zammito, *The Genesis of Kant's "Critique of Judgment,"* p. 46.

14 Crowther, *The Kantian Sublime*, p. 1. See also pp. 165–74.

15 Lyotard, *Lessons*, p. 75.

16 Kant, *Critique of Judgment*, p. 98.

17 Ibid., p. 99.

18 Kant, *Critique of Judgment*, p. 106. Brackets are translator's.

19 In *The Embodiment of Reason*, p. 216, Shell argues that in his "General Comment on the Exposition of Aesthetic Reflective Judgments," which immediately follows his discussion of the sublime, "Kant's description of the sublime now conflates the absolute magnitude formerly (uniquely) identified with the mathematical and the independence formerly (uniquely) identified with the dynamic." My argument is that they were already conflated in Kant's mind, and that the distinction is merely a heuristically provisional distinction.

20 Kant, *Critique of Judgment*, p. 119.

21 Ibid., p. 123.

22 Ibid., p. 123.

23 Ibid., p. 121.

24 See G.W.F. Hegel, *Science of Logic*, translated by A.V. Miller (London: George Allen & Unwin, 1969), pp. 106–7. Here Hegel identifies the essential component of sublation as a "lifting-up."

25 Rudolf A. Makkreel, *Imagination and Interpretation in Kant: The Hermeneutical Import of the "Critique of Judgment"* (Chicago: University of Chicago Press, 1990), p. 170.
26 For a critique of Makkreel, along with critiques of Crowther and Zammito, as well as a discussion of Lyotard, see Peter Fenves, "Taking Stock of the Kantian Sublime," *Eighteenth-Century Studies*, 28: 1, 1994, pp. 65–82.
27 Rudolf Makkreel, "Imagination and Temporality in Kant's Theory of the Sublime," *Journal of Aesthetics and Art Criticism* 42: 3, 1984, pp. 303–15.
28 Kant, *Critique of Judgment*, p. 108.
29 Ibid., p. 108.
30 Ibid., p. 109.
31 Ibid., p. 109.
32 Ibid., p. 109.
33 Ibid., p. 113.
34 Lyotard, *Lessons*, p. 138.
35 Kant, *Critique of Judgment*, p. 114.
36 Ibid., p. 119.
37 Kant, *Prolegomena*, p. 67. See also *Critique of Pure Reason*, A125–7.
38 Kant, *Critique of Judgment*, p. 125.
39 Ibid., p. 125.
40 Ibid., p. 121.
41 An interesting study, although beyond the scope of this work, would be an investigation of the way in which beauty and sublime are "coded" as feminine and masculine, respectively, and the effects of such gendered concepts on Kantian philosophy. Shell in *The Embodiment of Reason* devotes some attention to this topic (see pp. 219–24). Although Kant does not explicitly make such distinctions in the *Critique of Judgment*, in his 1763 work, *Observations on the Feeling of the Beautiful and the Sublime*, translated by John T. Goldthwait (Berkeley: University of California Press, 1960), he clearly identifies the beautiful with the female, and the male with the sublime. "The fair sex has just as much understanding as the male, but it is a beautiful understanding, whereas ours [sic!] should be a deep understanding, an expression that signifies identity with the sublime" (p. 78). Apparently the power and depth of the sublime are "masculine" in contrast to a frivolous and superficial "feminine" beauty. Such surface beauty is art or artful, also understood as artificial, while penetrating depth acquires the seriousness of morality. Kant continues to be interested in associating philosophical concepts (in very superficial ways) with empirical phenomena, all the way up to his *Anthropology from a Pragmatic Point of View*. A fascinating further complication is inserted by Slavoj Žižek, in his *Tarrying with the Negative: Kant, Hegel and the Critique of Ideology* (Durham: Duke University Press, 1993), pp. 53–4, who argues that "the split of the Sublime itself . . . into 'mathematical' and 'dynamic' . . . directly concerns sexual difference." Žižek claims that "prior to the opposition Sublime/Beautiful, sexual difference is inscribed in the inherent split of the Sublime into mathematical and dynamical." Žižek conducts a Lacanian reading of Kant (and Hegel) which I do not take up here, but his comment is suggestive to the extent that it aligns a feminine mathematical aspect with a considered masculine sublime. This coincidence is intriguing, since I take the mathematical sublime rather than the dynamical to be the representative case of the sublime.
42 Sallis, *Spacings*, p. 130.
43 Derrida, *The Truth in Painting*, p. 125.
44 Ibid., p. 143.
45 De Man, "Phenomenality and Materiality in Kant," p. 93.

46 Ibid., p. 107.
47 Kant, *Critique of Judgment*, p. 113.
48 Lyotard, *Lessons*, p. 113.
49 Sallis, *Spacings*, p. 98.
50 Ibid., p. 111.
51 See Kant, *Critique of Judgment*, p. 115. Pluhar translates: "This agitation . . . can be compared with a vibration, i.e., with a rapid alternation of repulsion from, and attraction to, one and the same object." This results in a disorientation. Sallis translates the term *Erschütterung* or vibration, however, as "tremoring" (*Spacings*, p. 126). This tremoring takes hold of the subject and spreads to encompass the object and becomes "an abyss in which imagination is afraid to lose itself." Sallis implicitly extends this tremoring to the entire Kantian critical project; I am trying to make that connection much more explicit.
52 Kant, *Critique of Judgment*, p. 111.
53 Lyotard, *Lessons*, p. 143.
54 Ibid., p. 143. Lyotard treats this topic of magnitude under the heading of "The Sublime as Dynamical Synthesis," even though Kant works out his understanding of sublime in relation to magnitude under the heading, "On the Mathematically Sublime."
55 Ibid., p. 144.
56 Ibid., p. 138.
57 Kant, *Critique of Judgment*, p. 108.
58 Lyotard, *Lessons*, p. 75.
59 Derrida, *The Truth in Painting*, p. 143.

6 The transcendental imagination

1 H.J. Paton writes that "the only category which we can legitimately apply to objects is the schematised category." *Kant's Metaphysics of Experience*, Vol. II, p. 68. Heidegger claims that "the formation of the schema is the making-sensible of concepts." *Kant and the Problem of Metaphysics*, p. 66.
2 In his article, "Kant's View of Imagination," (*Kant-Studien* 79, 1988, pp. 140–64), J. Michael Young comes close to concluding the former, combined with an attempt to give imagination its due, when he states that when employed by the understanding, imagination is "understood as the capacity to construe or interpret sensible awareness in accordance with general rules" (p. 163). Makkreel, in *Imagination and Interpretation in Kant*, attempts the latter, because it accords with his notion of hermeneutics, but Lyotard also partially neglects the importance of the *Critique of Pure Reason*.
3 Paton, *Kant's Metaphysics of Experience*, Vol. II, p. 25.
4 Schelling, *System of Transcendental Idealism*, p. 137.
5 W.H. Walsh, in his essay "Schematism" (in *Kant: A Collection of Critical Essays*, edited by Robert Paul Wolff, Notre Dame: University of Notre Dame Press, 1967, pp. 71–87), distinguishes between two different perspectives regarding the schema: the static and the dynamic (p. 77).
6 Charles E. Winquist, *The Transcendental Imagination: An Essay in Philosophical Theology* (The Hague: Martinus Nijhoff, 1972), p. 18.
7 Young, "Kant's View of Imagination," pp. 160–1.
8 Paton, *Kant's Metaphysics of Experience*, Vol. II, p. 36.
9 Ibid., p. 36.
10 Heidegger, *Kant and the Problem of Metaphysics*, p. 69.
11 Kant, *Critique of Judgment*, p. 225.
12 Ibid., p. 226.
13 Ibid., p. 227.

14 In "Schematism," pp. 84–5, Walsh writes that Kant implies that "every concept capable of schematisation can be schematised in only one way. The account of symbolisation, by contrast, seems to allow that the relationship between idea and symbol is altogether less intimate: symbolising is a relatively arbitrary process, and hence each idea can be symbolised in a variety of ways."

15 Kant, *Critique of Judgment*, p. 227.

16 Ibid., p. 227.

17 See Tillich, *Theology of Culture*, p. 54.

18 Kant, *Critique of Judgment*, p. 227.

19 Winquist, *The Transcendental Imagination*, p. 14.

20 Heidegger, *Kant and the Problem of Metaphysics*, p. 71.

21 Tillich, *Systematic Theology*, Vol. One, p. 165.

22 See Deleuze, *Difference and Repetition*, p. 86.

23 Gasché, *The Tain of the Mirror*, pp. 151–2.

24 See Alfred North Whitehead, *Process and Reality* (New York: The Free Press, 1978), p. 21.

25 Schelling, *System of Transcendental Idealism*, p. 143.

26 Ibid., p. 143.

27 Ibid., p. 143.

28 On Kant's distinction between thinking and knowing, see *Critique of Pure Reason*, Bxxvi and B146.

29 Deleuze, *Kant's Critical Philosophy*, p. vii.

30 Jacques Derrida, *Margins of Philosophy*, translated by Alan Bass (Chicago: University of Chicago Press, 1982).

31 Ibid., p. 8.

32 Ibid., p. 8.

33 Derrida, *Of Grammatology*, p. 10.

34 See Ferdinand de Saussure, *Course in General Linguistics*, translated by Roy Harris (LaSalle, Illinois: Open Court, 1986). Many linguists and other intellectuals influenced by Saussure have overlooked or dismissed the section on Diachronic Linguistics, seeing it as merely an appendage to structural synchronic analysis. Derrida introjects diachronic temporization into the heart of Saussure's system.

35 Derrida, *Of Grammatology*, p. 68.

36 Ibid., p. 290.

37 Derrida, *Margins of Philosophy*, p. 11.

38 Ibid., p. 27.

39 Ibid., pp. 4–5.

40 Derrida, *Of Grammatology*, pp. 290–1. On the replacement of a central framework of knowledge in terms of subject-object in Western intellectual thinking by one of self-other (more satisfying but not itself unproblematic), see Ray L. Hart, "Imagination and the Scale of Mental Acts," *Continuum*, III: 1, 1965, pp. 3–21.

41 Kevin Hart, *The Trespass of the Sign: Deconstruction, Theology, and Philosophy* (Cambridge: Cambridge University Press, 1989), p. 230.

42 See Deleuze, *Difference and Repetition*, p. 217, where differentiated spatial and temporal dynamisms underlie static or general concepts.

7 Towards a theology of the sublime

1 In *On Religion: Speeches to its Cultured Despisers*, translated by Richard Crouter (Cambridge: Cambridge University Press, 1988), Friedrich Schleiermacher claims, in his third speech "On Self Formation (*Bildung*) in Religion," that all communication of intuition is extremely difficult because it is indirect (p. 57).

2 Heidegger, *Being and Time*, p. 487.
3 Deleuze and Guattari, *What is Philosophy?*, p. 16. See also Paul Ricoeur, *Oneself as Another*, translated by Kathleen Blamey (Chicago: University of Chicago Press, 1992).
4 See Augustine, *The Confessions*, translated by Henry Chadwick (Oxford: Oxford University Press, 1991), and Peter Brown, *The Body and Society: Men, Women, and Sexual Renunciation in Early Christianity* (New York: Columbia University Press, 1988), pp. 387–427.
5 Jacques Derrida, *Aporias*, translated by Thomas Dutoit (Stanford: Stanford University Press, 1993), p. 77.
6 Ibid., pp. 76, 78.
7 Ibid., pp. 65, 79.
8 John Sallis, *The Gathering of Reason* (Athens, Ohio: Ohio University Press, 1980), p. 113.
9 On the topic of form in Kant, see Robert B. Pippin, *Kant's Theory of Form* (New Haven: Yale University Press, 1982), and Theodore E. Uehling, Jr., *The Notion of Form in Kant's Critique of Aesthetic Judgment* (The Hague: Mouton, 1971). While neither attends to the breaking of form which is represented by the sublime, Uehling suggests that in the sublime, "the object [is] either devoid of form or the form [is] such that it 'violated,' in some sense, human thought" (p. 72).
10 See Gilles Deleuze, *The Fold: Leibniz and the Baroque*, translated by Tom Conley (Minneapolis: University of Minnesota Press, 1993), for a study of the idea of thinking or subjectivity as a folding upon itself. In *Foucault*, translated by Seán Hand (Minneapolis: University of Minnesota Press, 1988), Deleuze argues that the interiority which marks subjectivity is actually a fold of an outside or external surface upon itself in order to create an "inside."
11 The idea of God "arises out of morality and is not its basis;" "for its own sake morality does not need religion at all," but "the man [sic] finds it needful:" "Morality thus ineluctably leads to religion." Kant, *Religion Within the Limits of Reason Alone*, translated by Theodore M. Greene and Hoyt H. Hudson (New York: Harper & Row, 1960), pp. 3–5.
12 Tillich, *Theology of Culture*, p. 7.
13 Ibid., p. 6.
14 Ibid., p. 7.
15 See Tillich, *Systematic Theology*, Vol. One, pp. 79–81.
16 Kant, *Critique of Judgment*, p. 115.
17 Deleuze, *Kant's Critical Philosophy*, p. 4.
18 Ibid., p. xii.
19 See Jonathan Z. Smith, *Imagining Religion: From Babylon to Jonestown* (Chicago: University of Chicago Press, 1982), although Smith would not use the term theology.
20 Winquist, *The Transcendental Imagination*, p. 5.
21 According to Thomas J.J. Altizer, Western theology is characterized by a vanishing of "every trace of a truly and finally transcendent God . . . and that vanishing is the realization of a pure and total immanence." *The Genesis of God: A Theological Genealogy* (Louisville: Westminster/John Knox Press, 1993), p. 21.
22 In Deleuze's *Difference and Repetition*, one can tentatively identify as a God-factor a logic of virtual differentiation, or what Deleuze sometimes calls the "dark precursor." See pp. 119, 123–4, 207, 217, and 222. Here Deleuze comes close to identifying God with the process or procedure of differentiation or schematism.
23 See Robert P. Scharlemann, "The Being of God when God is not Being God: Deconstructing the History of Theism," in *Inscriptions and Reflections*, edited

by Robert P. Scharlemann (Charlottesville: University of Virginia Press, 1989), pp. 31–53. For his development of the paradoxical concepts of religion and God in Tillich, see "Critical and Religious Consciousness: Some Reflections on the Question of Truth in the Philosophy of Religion," in *Kairos and Logos: Studies in the Roots and Implications of Tillich's Theology*, edited by John J. Carey (Atlanta: Mercer University Press, 1978), pp. 63–82.

24 Scharlemann, "The Being of God," p. 50.

25 See Thomas J.J. Altizer, *Total Presence* (New York: Seabury Press, 1980).

26 Ludwig Feuerbach, *The Essence of Christianity*, translated by George Eliot (Buffalo: Prometheus Books, 1989), p. xvii.

27 Friedrich Schleiermacher, *The Christian Faith*, edited by H.R. MacKintosh and J.S. Stewart (Edinburgh: T. & T. Clark, 1989), p. 16.

28 Paul Tillich, *Biblical Religion and the Search for Ultimate Reality* (Chicago: University of Chicago Press, 1955), p. 4.

29 See Wendy Farley, *Eros for the Other: Retaining Truth in a Pluralistic World* (University Park: Pennsylvania State University Press, 1996), and the collection of essays in *The Otherness of God (Studies in Religion and Culture)*, edited by Orrin F. Summerell (Charlottesville: University of Virginia Press, 1998).

30 See Sigmund Freud, *The Interpretation of Dreams*, translated by James Strachey (New York: Avon Books, 1965), Chapter VI, and Paul Ricoeur, *Freud and Philosophy: An Essay on Interpretation*, translated by Denis Savage (New Haven: Yale University Press, 1970).

31 See Sigmund Freud, "Formulations Regarding the Two Principles in Mental Functioning," in Sigmund Freud, *General Psychological Theory*, edited by Philip Rieff (New York: Macmillan, 1963), pp. 21–8.

32 According to Deleuze, this material plane cannot be thought of as a materialism which anchors the repetitions or substitutions of sublimity. See *Difference and Repetition*, pp. 104–5. According to Deleuze, we do not repeat because we repress, but we repress because we repeat—we repress the difference in thinking repetition is a repetition of identity.

33 Sigmund Freud, *The Standard Edition of the Complete Psychological Works*, Vol. XVII, translated and edited by James Strachey (London: The Hogarth Press, 1955), p. 238.

34 Sigmund Freud, *Beyond the Pleasure Principle*, translated and edited by James Strachey (New York: W.W. Norton, 1961), p. 46.

35 Ibid., p. 47.

36 Ibid., p. 47.

37 Carl A. Raschke, *Fire and Roses: Postmodernity and the Thought of the Body* (Albany: State University of New York Press, 1996), pp. 36–8.

38 Ibid., p. 51.

39 See Jacques Lacan, *The Four Fundamental Concepts of Psychoanalysis*, translated by Alan Sheridan (New York: W.W. Norton, 1978), p. 59.

40 Despite Christian constraints not to flee from the world, Blond turns away resoundingly from the messy actualities of empirical life to a majestically Platonic redeeming possibility. See "Introduction," *Post-Secular Philosophy*, pp. 21–9.

41 Two important such strategies are Julia Kristeva, *Revolution in Poetic Language*, translated by Margaret Waller (New York: Columbia University Press, 1984), and Gilles Deleuze, *The Logic of Sense*, translated by Mark Lester and Charles Stivale (New York: Columbia University Press, 1990).

42 See the essays by Derrida in the collection, *Derrida and Negative Theology*, edited by Harold Coward and Toby Foshay (Albany: State University of New York Press, 1992): "How to Avoid Speaking: Denials," "Of an Apocalyptic Tone Recently Adopted in Philosophy," and "Post-Scriptum: Aporias, Ways, Voices."

43 See Deleuze and Guattari, *What is Philosophy?* pp. 85–8.
44 The violence inherent in the sublime should not be overlooked, whether understood in the Kantian sense as developed here, or in a more Freudian cultural
sense. See Sigmund Freud, *Civilization and its Discontents*, translated by James
Strachey (New York: W.W. Norton, 1961). In *Eros and Civilization: A Philosophical Inquiry into Freud* (Boston: Beacon Press, 1956), Herbert Marcuse
focuses on the destruction of cultural sublimation (which is not to ignore the
violence inherent in individual sublimation): "Culture demands continuous sublimation; it thereby weakens Eros, the builder of culture. And desexualization,
by weakening Eros, unbinds the destructive impulses" (p. 83).

Bibliography

Allison, Henry E. *The Kant–Eberhard Controversy*. Baltimore: Johns Hopkins University Press, 1973.

Allison, Henry E. *Kant's Transcendental Idealism: An Interpretation and Defense*. New Haven: Yale University Press, 1983.

Altizer, Thomas J.J. *The Genesis of God: A Theological Genealogy*. Louisville: Westminster/John Knox Press, 1993.

Altizer, Thomas J.J. *Total Presence*. New York: Seabury Press, 1980.

Ameriks, Karl and Dieter Sturma, eds. *The Modern Subject: Conceptions of the Self in Classical German Philosophy*. Albany: State University of New York Press, 1995.

Arendt, Hannah. *Eichmann in Jerusalem: A Report on the Banality of Evil*. New York: Viking Press, 1963.

Asad, Talal. *Genealogies of Religion*. Baltimore: Johns Hopkins University Press, 1993.

Augustine. *The Confessions*, translated by Henry Chadwick. Oxford: Oxford University Press, 1991.

Balthasar, Hans Urs von. *The Glory of the Lord: A Theological Aesthetics*, Volume II: *Studies in Theological Style: Clerical Styles*, translated by Andrew Louth, Francis McDonagh, and Brian McNeil. Edinburgh: T. & T. Clark, 1984.

Barth, Karl. *The Word of God and the Word of Man*, translated by Douglas Horton. Gloucester, Mass.: Peter Smith, 1978.

Beck, Lewis White. *Early German Philosophy: Kant and His Predecessors*. Cambridge, Mass.: Harvard University Press, 1969.

Benhabib, Selya. *Situating the Self: Gender, Community, and Postmodernism in Contemporary Ethics*. New York: Routledge, 1992.

Bennett, Jonathan. *Kant's Analytic*. Cambridge: Cambridge University Press, 1966.

Bergson, Henri. *The Creative Mind*, translated by Mabelle L. Andison. New York: Philosophical Library, 1946.

Bergson, Henri. *An Introduction to Metaphysics*, translated by T.E. Hulme. New York: Macmillan, 1955.

Blocker, Harry. "Kant's Theory of the Relation of Imagination and Understanding in Aesthetic Judgments of Taste." *British Journal of Aesthetics*, 5: 1, 1965, pp. 37–45.

Blond, Phillip, ed. *Post-Secular Philosophy: Between Philosophy and Theology*. London: Routledge, 1998.

Bouwsma, William J. *John Calvin: A Sixteenth Century Portrait*. New York: Oxford University Press, 1988.

Brown, Peter. *The Body and Society: Men, Women and Sexual Renunciation in Early Christianity*. New York: Columbia University Press, 1988.

Calvin, John. *Institutes of the Christian Religion*, edited by John T. McNeill and translated by Ford Lewis Battles. Philadelphia: Westminster Press, 1960.

Canning, Peter. "Jesus Christ Holocaust: Fabulation of the Jews in Christian and Nazi History." *Journal for Cultural and Religious Theory*, 1: 2, April 2000, www.jcrt.org.

Carl, Wolfgang. "Kant's First Drafts of the Deduction of the Categories." In *Kant's Transcendental Deductions: The Three Critiques and the Opus Postumum*, edited by Eckart Förster. Stanford: Stanford University Press, 1989.

Cassirer, Ernst. *Kant's Life and Thought*, translated by James Haden. New Haven: Yale University Press, 1981.

Copleston, Frederick. *A History of Philosophy*. Volume VI: *Wolff to Kant*. Westminster, Md: The Newman Press, 1961.

Coward, Harold and Toby Foshay, eds. *Derrida and Negative Theology*. Albany: State University of New York Press, 1992.

Crockett, Clayton. "On the Disorientation of the Study of Religion." In *What is Religion? Origins, Definitions & Explanations*, edited by Thomas A. Idinopulos and Brian C. Wilson. Leiden: Brill, 1998.

Crossan, J.D. *The Historical Jesus: The Life of a Jewish Mediterranean Peasant*. San Francisco: HarperCollins, 1991.

Crowther, Paul. *The Kantian Sublime: From Morality to Art*. Oxford: Clarendon Press, 1989.

Cutrofello, Andrew. *Discipline and Critique: Kant, Poststructuralism, and the Problem of Resistance*. Albany: State University of New York Press, 1994.

Cutrofello, Andrew. *Imagining Otherwise: Metapsychology and the Analytic A Posteriori*. Evanston: Northwestern University Press, 1997.

Davidovich, Adina. *Religion as a Province of Meaning: The Kantian Foundations of Modern Theology*. Minneapolis: Fortress Press, 1993.

de Man, Paul. "Phenomenality and Materiality in Kant." In *The Textual Sublime: Deconstruction and its Differences*, edited by Hugh J. Silverman and Gary E. Aylesworth. Albany: State University of New York Press, 1990.

Deleuze, Gilles. *Bergsonism*, translated by Hugh Tomlinson and Barbara Habberjam. New York: Zone Books, 1991.

Deleuze, Gilles. *Difference and Repetition*, translated by Paul Patton. New York: Columbia University Press, 1994.

Deleuze, Gilles. *The Fold: Leibniz and the Baroque*, translated by Tom Conley. Minneapolis: University of Minnesota Press, 1993.

Deleuze, Gilles. *Foucault*, translated by Seán Hand. Minneapolis: University of Minnesota Press, 1988.

Deleuze, Gilles. *Kant's Critical Philosophy*, translated by Hugh Tomlinson and Barbara Habberjam. Minneapolis: University of Minnesota Press, 1984.

Deleuze, Gilles. *The Logic of Sense*, translated by Mark Lester and Charles Stivale. New York: Columbia University Press, 1990.

Deleuze, Gilles and Félix Guattari. *What is Philosophy?* translated by Hugh Tomlinson and Graham Burchell. New York: Columbia University Press, 1994.

Derrida, Jacques. *Aporias*, translated by Thomas Dutoit. Stanford: Stanford University Press, 1993.

Derrida, Jacques. *Margins of Philosophy*, translated by Alan Bass. Chicago: University of Chicago Press, 1982.

Derrida, Jacques. *Of Grammatology*, translated by Gayatri Chakravorty Spivak. Baltimore: Johns Hopkins University Press, 1976.

Derrida, Jacques. *The Other Heading: Reflections on Today's Europe*, translated by Pascale-Anne Brault and Michael B. Naas. Bloomington: Indiana University Press, 1992.

Derrida, Jacques. *The Truth in Painting*, translated by Geoff Bennington and Ian McLeod. Chicago: University of Chicago Press, 1987.

Dufrenne, Mikel. *In the Presence of the Sensuous: Essays in Aesthetics*, edited by Mark S. Roberts and Dennis Gallagher. Atlantic Highlands, NJ: Humanities Press International, 1987.

Ewing, A.C. *A Short Commentary on Kant's "Critique of Pure Reason."* Chicago: University of Chicago Press, 1967.

Fackenheim, Emil. *The God Within: Kant, Schelling, and Historicity*, edited by John Burbidge. Toronto: University of Toronto Press, 1996.

Farley, Wendy. *Eros for the Other: Retaining Truth in a Pluralistic World.* University Park: Pennsylvania State University Press, 1996.

Fenves, Peter D. *A Peculiar Fate: Metaphysics and World-History in Kant.* Ithaca: Cornell University Press, 1991.

Fenves, Peter D. "Taking Stock of the Kantian Sublime." *Eighteenth-Century Studies*, 28: 1, 1994, pp. 65–82.

Feuerbach, Ludwig. *The Essence of Christianity*, translated by George Eliot. Buffalo: Prometheus Books, 1989.

Fichte, J.G. *Science of Knowledge*, translated by Peter Heath. New York: Cambridge University Press, 1982.

Förster, Eckart, ed. *Kant's Transcendental Deductions: The Three Critiques and the Opus Postumum.* Stanford: Stanford University Press, 1989.

Foucault, Michel. *The Order of Things: An Archaeology of the Human Sciences.* New York: Vintage Books, 1973.

Freud, Sigmund. *Beyond the Pleasure Principle*, translated and edited by James Strachey. New York: W.W. Norton, 1961.

Freud, Sigmund. *Civilization and Its Discontents*, translated by James Strachey. New York: W.W. Norton, 1961.

Freud, Sigmund. *General Psychological Theory*, edited by Philip Rieff. New York: Macmillan, 1963.

Freud, Sigmund. *The Interpretation of Dreams*, translated by James Strachey. New York: Avon Books, 1965.

Freud, Sigmund. "The Uncanny." in *The Standard Edition of the Complete Psychological Works of Sigmund Freud*, Volume XVII, translated by James Strachey. London: The Hogarth Press, 1955.

Gasché, Rodolphe. *The Tain of the Mirror: Derrida and the Philosophy of Reflection.* Cambridge: Harvard University Press, 1986.

Gell-Mann, Murray, *The Quark and the Jaguar: Adventures in the Simple and the Complex.* New York: W.H. Freeman and Co., 1994.

Gibbons, Sarah L. *Kant's Theory of Imagination: Bridging Gaps in Judgment and Experience.* Oxford: Clarendon Press, 1994.

Goetschel, Willi. *Constituting Critique: Kant's Writing as Critical Praxis*, translated by Eric Schwab. Durham: Duke University Press, 1994.

Guyer, Paul. *Kant and the Claims of Knowledge*. Cambridge: Cambridge University Press, 1987.

Habermas, Jürgen. *Postmetaphysical Thinking: Philosophical Essays*, translated by William Mark Hohengarten. Cambridge, Mass.: MIT Press, 1992.

Hart, Kevin. *The Trespass of the Sign: Deconstruction, Theology, and Philosophy*. Cambridge: Cambridge University Press, 1989.

Hart, Ray L. "Imagination and the Scale of Mental Acts." *Continuum* III: I, 1965, pp. 3–21.

Hedley, Douglas, "Should Divinity Overcome Metaphysics? Reflections on John Milbank's Theology Beyond Secular Reason and Confessions of a Cambridge Platonist." *Journal of Religion* 80: 2, April 2000, pp. 271–98.

Hegel, G.W.F. *Phenomenology of Spirit*, translated by A.V. Miller. Oxford: Oxford University Press, 1977.

Hegel, G.W.F. *Science of Logic*, translated by A.V. Miller. London: George Allen & Unwin, 1969.

Heidegger, Martin. *Being and Time*, translated by John Macquarrie and Edward Robinson. New York: Harper & Row, 1962.

Heidegger, Martin. *Kant and the Problem of Metaphysics*, translated by Richard Taft. Bloomington: Indiana University Press, 1990.

Heidegger, Martin. *Nietzsche*. Volumes One and Two, translated by David Farrell Krell. San Francisco: HarperCollins, 1991.

Heidegger, Martin. *Phenomenological Interpretation of Kant's "Critique of Pure Reason,"* translated by Parvis Emad and Kenneth Maly. Bloomington: Indiana University Press, 1997.

Henrich, Dieter. *Aesthetic Judgment and the Moral Image of the World: Studies in Kant*. Stanford: Stanford University Press, 1992.

Henrich, Dieter. *Identität und Objectivität: Eine Untersuchung über Kants transzendentale Deduktion*. Heidelberg: Carl Winter Universitätsverlag, 1976.

Henrich, Dieter. "Kant's Notion of a Deduction and the Methodological Background of the First *Critique*." In *Kant's Transcendental Deductions: The Three Critiques and the Opus Postumum*, edited by Eckart Förster. Stanford: Stanford University Press, 1989.

Henrich, Dieter. "The Proof-Structure of Kant's Transcendental Deduction." *Review of Metaphysics* 22: 4, 1969, pp. 640–59.

Horkheimer, Max and Theodor W. Adorno. *Dialectic of Enlightenment*, translated by John Cumming. New York: Continuum, 1993.

Huizinga, Johann. *Erasmus and the Age of Reformation*. New York: Harper & Row, 1957.

Hume, David. *An Inquiry Concerning Human Understanding*. Buffalo: Prometheus Books, 1988.

Ingram, David. "The Postmodern Kantianism of Arendt and Lyotard." *Review of Metaphysics* 42, 1988, pp. 51–77.

Jaspers, Karl. *Kant*, translated by Ralph Manheim. New York: Harcourt Brace Jovanovich, 1962.

Kant, Immanuel. *Anthropology from a Pragmatic Point of View*, translated by Mary J. Gregor. The Hague: Martinus Nijhoff, 1974.

Kant, Immanuel. *The Conflict of the Faculties*, translated by Mary J. Gregor. Lincoln: University of Nebraska Press, 1979.

Kant, Immanuel. *Critique of Judgment*, translated by Werner Pluhar. Indianapolis: Hackett Publishing Company, 1987.

Kant, Immanuel. *Critique of Practical Reason*, translated by Lewis White Beck. New Jersey: Prentice-Hall, 1993.

Kant, Immanuel. *Critique of Pure Reason*, translated by Norman Kemp Smith. New York: St Martin's Press, 1965.

Kant, Immanuel. *Immanuel Kants Werke*, edited by Ernst Cassirer. Band III, *Kritik Der Reinen Vernuft*. Berlin: Bruno Cassirer, 1922.

Kant, Immanuel. *Kant: Philosophical Correspondence 1759–99*, edited and translated by Arnulf Zweig. Chicago: University of Chicago Press, 1967.

Kant, Immanuel. *Observations on the Feeling of the Beautiful and Sublime*, translated by John T. Goldthwait. Berkeley: University of California Press, 1960.

Kant, Immanuel. *Opus Postumum*, translated by Eckart Förster and Michael Rosen. Cambridge: Cambridge University Press, 1993.

Kant, Immanuel. *Prolegomena to Any Future Metaphysics*, translated by Lewis White Beck. Indianapolis: Bobbs-Merrill Company, Inc., 1950.

Kant, Immanuel. *Raising the Tone of Philosophy: Late Essays by Immanuel Kant, Transformative Critique by Jacques Derrida*, edited by Peter Fenves. Baltimore: Johns Hopkins University Press, 1993.

Kant, Immanuel. *Religion Within Limits of Reason Alone*, translated by Theodore M. Greene and Hoyt H. Hudson. New York: Harper & Row, 1960.

Kant, Immanuel. *Theoretical Philosophy: 1755–1770*, translated and edited by David Walford and Ralf Meerbote. Cambridge: Cambridge University Press, 1992.

Kant, Immanuel. "What is Orientation in Thinking?" translated by H.B. Nisbet, in *Kant: Political Writings*, edited by Hans Reiss. Cambridge: Cambridge University Press, 1991.

Kearney, Richard. *The Wake of Imagination: Toward a Postmodern Culture*. Minneapolis: University of Minnesota Press, 1988.

Kemp Smith, Norman. *A Commentary on Kant's "Critique of Pure Reason."* New York: Humanities Press, 1962.

Kristeva, Julia. *Revolution in Poetic Language*, translated by Margaret Waller. New York: Columbia University Press, 1984.

Lacan, Jacques. *The Four Fundamental Concepts of Psychoanalysis*, translated by Alan Sheridan. New York: W.W. Norton, 1978.

Lebrun, Gérard. *Kant et la mort de la métaphysique: Essai sur la "Critique de la faculté de Juger."* Paris: Librairie Armand Colin, 1970.

Lessing, G.E. *Lessing's Theological Writings*, translated by Henry Chadwick. Stanford: Stanford University Press, 1957.

Long, Charles H. *Significations: Signs, Symbols, and Images in the Interpretation of Religion*. Philadelphia: Fortress Press, 1986.

Luther, Martin. "The Freedom of a Christian," translated by W.A. Lambert, in *Martin Luther: Three Treatises*. Philadelphia: Fortress Press, 1970.

Luther, Martin. *Martin Luther: Selections from his Writings*, edited by John Dillenberger. New York: Doubleday, 1962.

Lyotard, Jean-François. *The Differend: Phrases in Dispute*, translated by Georges Van Den Abeele. Minneapolis: University of Minnesota Press, 1988.

Lyotard, Jean-François. *Heidegger and "the jews,"* translated by Andreas Michel and Mark S. Roberts. Minneapolis: University of Minnesota Press, 1990.

Lyotard, Jean-François. *Lessons on the Analytic of the Sublime*, translated by Elizabeth Rottenberg. Stanford: Stanford University Press, 1994.

Lyotard, Jean François and Jean Thebault. *Just Gaming*, translated by Wlad Godzich and Brian Massumi. Minneapolis: University of Minnesota Press, 1985.

MacIntyre, Alasdair. *After Virtue: A Study in Moral Theory*. 2nd ed. Notre Dame: University of Notre Dame Press, 1997.

MacIntyre, Alasdair. *Three Rival Versions of Moral Enquiry: Encyclopedia Genealogy and Tradition*. Notre Dame: University of Notre Dame Press, 1990.

Makkreel, Rudolf A. *Imagination and Interpretation in Kant: The Hermeneutical Import of the "Critique of Judgment."* Chicago: University of Chicago Press, 1990.

Makkreel, Rudolf A. "Imagination and Temporality in Kant's Theory of the Sublime." *Journal of Aesthetics and Art Criticism* 42: 3, 1984, pp. 303–15.

Marcuse, Herbert. *Eros and Civilization: A Philosophical Inquiry into Freud*. Boston: Beacon Press, 1956.

Marion, Jean-Luc. "God and Onto-Theology," translated by Bettina Bergo. In *Post-Secular Philosophy: Between Philosophy and Theology*, edited by Phillip Blond. London: Routledge, 1998.

Marion, Jean-Luc. *God Without Being: Hors-texte*, translated by Thomas A. Carlson. Chicago: University of Chicago Press, 1991.

Marion, Jean-Luc. *Reduction and Givenness: Investigations of Husserl, Heidegger, and Phenomenology*, translated by Thomas A. Carlson. Evanston: Northwestern University Press, 1998.

Melnick, Arthur. *Space, Time, and Thought in Kant*. Dordrecht, Netherlands: Kluwer Academic Publishers, 1989.

Milbank, John. *Theology and Social Theory: Beyond Secular Reason*. Oxford: Blackwell, 1990.

Milbank, John. *The Word Made Strange: Theology, Language, Culture*. Cambridge, Mass.: Blackwell, 1997.

Milbank, John, Catherine Pickstock, and Graham Ward, eds. *Radical Orthodoxy: A New Theology*. London: Routledge, 1999.

Mohanty, J.N., and Robert W. Shahan, eds. *Essays on Kant's Critique of Pure Reason*. Norman: University of Oklahoma Press, 1982.

Nietzsche, Friedrich. *Beyond Good and Evil*, translated by Walter Kaufmann. New York: Vintage Books, 1966.

Nietzsche, Friedrich. *Ecce Homo*, translated by R.J. Hollingdale. London: Penguin Books, 1979.

Otto, Rudolf. *The Idea of the Holy*, translated by John W. Harvey. New York: Oxford University Press, 1950.

Paton, H.J. *Kant's Metaphysics of Experience*. 2 volumes. London: George Allen & Unwin Ltd., 1951.

Pickstock, Catherine. *After Writing: On the Liturgical Consummation of Philosophy*. Oxford: Blackwell, 1998.

Pippin, Robert B. *Kant's Theory of Form*. New Haven: Yale University Press, 1982.

Raschke, Carl A. *Fire and Roses: Postmodernity and the Thought of the Body*. Albany: State University of New York Press, 1996.

Ricoeur, Paul. *Freud and Philosophy: An Essay on Interpretation*, translated by Denis Savage. New Haven: Yale University Press, 1970.

Ricoeur, Paul. *Oneself as Another*, translated by Kathleen Blamey. Chicago: University of Chicago Press, 1992.

Roberts, Tyler T. *Contesting Spirit: Nietzsche, Affirmation, Religion*. Princeton: Princeton University Press, 1998.

Sallis, John. *The Gathering of Reason*. Athens, Ohio: Ohio University Press, 1980.

Sallis, John. *Spacings—Of Reason and Imagination in Texts of Kant, Fichte, Hegel*. Chicago: University of Chicago Press, 1987.

Sallis, John. *Stone*. Bloomington: Indiana University Press, 1994.

Saussure, Ferdinand de. *Course in General Linguistics*, translated by Roy Harris. LaSalle, Illinois: Open Court, 1986.

Schalow, Frank. *The Renewal of the Heidegger–Kant Dialogue: Action, Thought and Responsibility*. Albany: State University of New York Press, 1992.

Scharlemann, Robert P. "The Being of God When God is Not Being God: Deconstructing the History of Theism." In *Inscriptions and Reflections*, edited by Robert P. Scharlemann. Charlottesville: University Press of Virginia, 1989.

Scharlemann, Robert P. "Critical and Religious Consciousness: Some Reflections on the Question of Truth in the Philosophy of Religion." In *Kairos and Logos: Studies in the Roots and Implications of Tillich's Theology*, edited by John J. Carey. Atlanta: Mercer University Press, 1978.

Scharlemann, Robert P., ed. *Theology at the End of the Century: A Dialogue on the Postmodern with Thomas J.J. Altizer, Mark C. Taylor, Charles E. Winquist, and Robert P. Scharlemann*. Charlottesville: University of Virginia Press, 1990.

Schelling, F.W.J. *System of Transcendental Idealism*, translated by Peter Heath. Charlottesville: University of Virginia Press, 1978.

Schleiermacher, F.D.E. *The Christian Faith*, edited by H.R. MacKintosh and J.S. Stewart. Edinburgh: T. & T. Clark, 1989.

Schleiermacher, F.D.E. *On Religion: Speeches to its Cultured Despisers*, translated by Richard Crouter. Cambridge: Cambridge University Press, 1988.

Schnädelbach, Herbert. *Philosophy in Germany: 1831–1933*, translated by Eric Matthews. Cambridge: Cambridge University Press, 1984.

Shell, Susan Meld. *The Embodiment of Reason: Kant on Spirit, Generation, and Community*. Chicago: University of Chicago Press, 1996.

Sherover, Charles M. *Heidegger, Kant, and Time*. Bloomington: Indiana University Press, 1971.

Smith, Jonathan Z. *Imagining Religion: From Babylon to Jonestown*. Chicago: University of Chicago Press, 1982.

Sondregger, Katherine. *That Jesus Christ Was Born a Jew: Karl Barth's "Doctrine of Israel."* University Park: Pennsylvania State University Press, 1992.

Strawson, P.F. *The Bounds of Sense: An Essay on Kant's "Critique of Pure Reason."* London: Methuen & Co. Ltd., 1966.

Summerell, Orrin F., ed. *The Otherness of God (Studies in Religion and Culture)*. Charlottesville: University of Virginia Press, 1998.

Taylor, Charles. *Sources of the Self: The Making of Modern Identity*. Cambridge, Mass.: Harvard University Press, 1989.

Taylor, Mark C. *Erring: A Postmodern A/theology*. Chicago: University of Chicago Press, 1984.

Tillich, Paul. *Biblical Religion and the Search for Ultimate Reality*. Chicago: University of Chicago Press, 1955.

Tillich, Paul. *Dynamics of Faith*. New York: Harper & Row, 1957.

Tillich, Paul. *Systematic Theology*. 3 volumes. Chicago: University of Chicago Press, 1951.

Tillich, Paul. *Theology of Culture*. Oxford: Oxford University Press, 1959.

Toulmin, Stephen. *Cosmopolis: The Hidden Agenda of Modernity*. Chicago: University of Chicago Press, 1992.

Uehling, Theodore E., Jr. *The Notion of Form in Kant's Critique of Aesthetic Judgment*. The Hague: Mouton, 1971.

Vahanian, Gabriel. *God and Utopia*. New York: The Seabury Press, 1977.

Vahanian, Gabriel. *L'utopie chrétienne*. Paris: Desclée de Brouwer, 1992.

Vattimo, Gianni. *The End of Modernity*, translated by Jon R. Snyder. Baltimore: Johns Hopkins University Press, 1988.

Vattimo, Gianni. *The Transparent Society*, translated by David Webb. Baltimore: Johns Hopkins University Press, 1992.

Walsh, W.H. "Schematism." In *Kant: A Collection of Critical Essays*, edited by Robert Paul Wolff, pp. 71–87. Notre Dame: University of Notre Dame Press, 1967.

Ward, Graham. *Barth, Derrida and the Language of Theology*. Cambridge: Cambridge University Press, 1995.

Whitehead, Alfred North. *Process and Reality*. New York: The Free Press, 1978.

Wilken, Robert. *The Christians as the Romans Saw Them*. New Haven: Yale University Press, 1986.

Winquist, Charles E. *Desiring Theology*. Chicago: University of Chicago Press, 1995.

Winquist, Charles E. *The Transcendental Imagination: An Essay in Philosophical Theology*. The Hague: Martinus Nijhoff, 1972.

Young, Michael J. "Kant's View of Imagination." *Kant-Studien* 79, 1988, pp. 140–64.

Zammito, John H. *The Genesis of Kant's "Critique of Judgment."* Chicago: University of Chicago Press, 1992.

Zanetti, Veronique. "Teleology and the Freedom of the Self." In *The Modern Subject: Conceptions of the Self in Classical German Philosophy*, edited by Karl Ameriks and Dieter Sturma. Albany: State University of New York Press, 1995.

Žižek, Slavoj. *Tarrying with the Negative: Kant, Hegel and the Critique of Ideology*. Durham: Duke University Press, 1993.

Index

aesthetics: artistic 67; Balthasar 31–2;
    Kantian 32, 44–5, 48, 67–71, 83;
    lack of objective judgment 49,
    69–71, 80, 83
Allison, Henry 2
Altizer, Thomas J.J. 25, 107
Andenken 20
Anglicanism: and Aquinas 23
Anselm 106
anthropology 5, 108
anti-semitism: historical 26
aporia(s) 23, 29, 34, 73, 101–2
Aquinas, Thomas 6, 23–4, 27, 29
Arendt, Hannah 49
Aristophanes (myth of) 111
Aristotle 6, 24, 25
Augustine (of Hippo) 6, 24, 25, 100–1
Auschwitz 48

Balthasar, Hans Urs von 31–2
Barth, Karl: *Church Dogmatics* 31;
    obligation and difficulty of speaking
    of God 35; restriction of authentic
    theologizing to the churches 5
beauty: aesthetic judgment 19, 69–71,
    80, 83; divine 31–3; Kant's doctrine
    of 44, 69–71, 89, 110; and logic
    31–2
Benhabib, Seyla 11
Benjamin, Walter 18
Bennett, Jonathan 2
Bergson, Henri 54, 96
Berkeley, George 34
Bible and scripture: literality
    challenged by German critical
    Enlightenment 15–16; locus of
    authority 15
Blond, Phillip 23, 29–30
Buddhism: theology? 35–6

Calvin, John 16
causality: Hume 14–15
Christianity: defined in opposition to
    Judaism 26; idealization of
    premodern society 24–5; Trinity 33;
    and violence 24–7
Cicero 16
comfort: desire for 5–6
cross: significance of 26–7
Crowther, Paul 70
culture: Rousseau 68; study of "other"
    cultures 108; and sublime in nature
    76; Tillich 4, 102

de Man, Paul 78
death 37, 55, 101
death drive 110–11
Death of God theology 5, 9, 63,
    106–7
Deleuze, Gilles: conflict of the faculties
    (Kant) 4, 45–6, 48, 93; difference or
    differentiation 4, 32, 33, 63, 98;
    higher forms (of faculties) 104–5;
    imagination 44; Kant 2, 3, 62–5;
    questioning of philosophy 6, 33;
    Radical Orthodoxy and 23, 34;
    subjectivity 11, 100; task of
    philosophy 22; time and self 62–5,
    81, 83, 95
Derrida, Jacques: aporia 101; conflicts
    among the faculties 84; *différance*
    ix, 4, 95–8; effect of Kant on 2, 3,
    34; Gasché on 93; logic of
    supplementarity and exemplarity 68;
    Of Grammatology 96; questioning
    of philosophy 6; Radical Orthodoxy
    and 23, 27, 34; Rousseau and
    supplement 67–8; status of the
    "Other" 108; subjectivity 11;

sublime 67–8, 77, 83, 97; time and space 96–7
Descartes, René: cogito 29–30, 56, 107–8; continuity with Kant 30; *Meditations* 26, 29; paradigmatic figure 14; self 9, 10
differend: Lyotard's model 45–6, 48–9
Dilthey, Wilhelm: hermeneutics 74
disorientation: formal theology of 20; and Kantian sublime 19, 28, 110; value to theology ix, 17–18, 104–5, 112
duration (Bergson) 54

ego *see* self
Eichmann, Adolf 49
empirical intuition 58, 59, 79, 81, 85–6
empirical realism (Kant) 51–3, 55–7
Enlightenment: confidence in reason x, 77; influenced by Reformation (Catholic and Protestant) 25–6; modern inheritance 24–5
Erasmus 15
eschatology: Vahanian's theology 21
ethics: philosophical 23–4; and violence 32; *see also* morality
evil: Rousseau 68
Ewing, A.C. 55
existentialism: modern liberal dilemma 24; religious experience 11–12
experience: empirical 53, 57, 62; interrogation of limits of 27–8; phenomenal 27; subjective 53; textual 22; transcendental/ ontological knowledge 38–9; *see also* empirical realism; religious experience

faith: confused with piety 5–6; foundation for 23; knife edge between faith and doubt 27
Feuerbach, Ludwig 107–8
Foucault, Michel 10, 25
freedom: and morality 46
Freud, Sigmund 109–11

Garve, Christian: Kant's letter to 52
Gasché, Rudolphe 27, 93
Genet, Jean 34
God: Anselm's definition 106; Barth on 35; death of God theology 5, 9, 63, 106–7; Derridan view 34; Descartes and 29–30; and

imagination 91; Kantian view 30–1, 63; of love 32; mystery of (unknowable) 29, 32, 108; negative expression 106; objective center for orientation 17, 30; reconceptualized as *cogitatio* 30; replaced by self 100, 107; reunion of thinking and power 30–2; search of religious texts for ideas of 3; transcendental ideas of 3, 12–13, 30; ultimate concern 12; the unconscious 111
Goetschel, Willi 59
Gregory of Nyssa 25
Guattari, Félix 2, 33, 100
Guyer, Paul 2, 56

Habermas, Jürgen 14, 107
Hamlet 62
Hamann, J.G. 34
harmony: depends on teleological order 33
Hart, Kevin 97
Hauerwas, Stanley 16
Hedley, Douglas 25, 33
Hegel, G.W.F. 9, 25, 34, 73, 74, 77, 93, 107
Heidegger, Martin: *Being and Time* 11, 38–42, 50, 99; care 38; *Dasein* 3, 10, 37–9, 42, 99–101; imagination 73, 74, 91; and Kant 2, 3, 37–44, 50, 58–62, 63, 89; *Kant and the Problem of Metaphysics* 39, 42, 44, 50; Lyotard 50; notion of a blow 18; Radical Orthodoxy and 23, 34; rereading by Marion 35; subjectivity 11, 42, 50, 100; time and temporality 3, 38, 53, 57, 82, 92; tradition 20
Henrich, Dieter 56, 59, 63–4, 69–70
Hobbes, Thomas 24
Holocaust: betrayal or fulfilment of Enlightment ideals 25; Christian complicity? 26; failure of reason to prevent 77; Lyotard's differend theory 48–9
Holy: contemporary secular theology not opposed to 21; dissolution in modernity 105–7; Otto's idea of 19
Hume, David ix, 14–15
Husserl, E.G.A. 35, 97

idolatry: determinate object as ultimate concern 12; risk for theology 12, 35

imagination: conflict with reason 4,
71–83; destructive power of 75–6,
78; difficulties with infinity 49,
103–4; disruption of representation
92; epistemological 91; Makkreel
73–4; negative x, 73, 74, 83, 91–2,
98; place of 39–44, 49–50, 58–65,
69–70; to relate concepts and
intuitions 39, 86–9, 93; and
understanding 39, 43, 59, 64, 82,
86, 94; *see also* transcendental
imagination
immortality: personal 55
infinity 49, 74–6, 78–81, 83, 104
intuition: aesthetic absolute magnitude
75; empirical 58, 59, 79, 81, 85–6;
inner and outer 94–5; Lyotard 45,
47; reflective judgment 69–70;
schema 87–95; sensible 39–42, 57;
sensory 79; successive 53; synthesis
55–8, 60–1, 79; time and space
13–14, 52–3

Jacobi, F.H. 17
Jesus Christ: crucifixion 26
Judaism: opposed by Christianity 26;
see also Holocaust
judgment: aesthetic 44–5, 48–9,
68–71, 80, 83; determinative 85;
disappearance of understanding
78–83; practised not taught 58;
reason legislates overall 48–9; rules
for (schematism) 85–6, 90; sublime
4, 48–9, 75, 77, 80, 83–4

Kant, Immanuel: aesthetics 19, 32,
67–71, 83; Analogies of Experience
57; *Anthropology from a Pragmatic
Point of View* 108; beauty 44,
69–71, 110; conflict of the faculties
x, 4, 32, 45–6, 48, 64–5, 83–4, 93;
"Copernican revolution" 2, 37–8,
105; critical philosophy as theology
9–22; Critique of all Theology 106;
Critique of Judgment ix, 3–4, 18,
22, 37, 44–50, 51, 65, 67–84,
85–90, 98, 103; *Critique of
Practical Reason* 46, 48; *Critique
of Pure Reason* ix, 2–4, 12, 14, 19,
22, 37–40, 42, 45–50, 51–3, 58–65,
67–84, 85–6, 88, 99, 107; Deleuze
2, 3, 62–5; Derrida 2, 3, 34, 68;
empiricism 14, 39, 51–3, 55–7, 63,

79; and God 30–1, 63; Heidegger
2, 3, 37–44, 50, 58–62, 63;
imagination 39–44, 58–65, 70–1;
knowing experience 14, 38, 57;
Lyotard's interpretation of 44–50;
mathematics 81, 83; metaphysician
and metaphorician 2–3;
methodology 21–2; objects 15;
ontology 37–44; *Opus Postumum*
1; orientation 17–18; paradigmatic
thinker of modernity 2, 6, 10;
*Prolegomena to any Future
Metaphysics* 15, 76; Radical
Orthodoxy enemy to 27–31; reason
17–18, 23, 29, 43, 52, 55, 63, 102;
Schematism 4, 22, 37, 40–3, 50,
56–8, 61, 65, 70, 78, 83–95, 98,
99, 102; self 11, 38, 62–5; self-
consciousness 38, 42, 54–8;
subjectivity 53, 55–8, 69; sublime
3–5, 17–19, 22, 28–31, 44–5, 49,
50, 65, 67–84, 98, 103–4, 109–12;
temporality and spatiality 37,
52–65, 96–7; Transcendental
Aesthetic 13, 52, 54, 64, 67, 82;
transcendental arguments 27, 29,
35, 38–44, 65; Transcendental
Deduction 4, 39, 54–62, 64, 70,
79–80, 86, 99; transcendental ego
9, 63; transcendental idealism 15,
94–5; transcendental imagination
39, 43, 51–2, 57–8, 58–62, 83–4,
85–98; Transcendental Schematism
22, 40–1, 86; ultimate concern ix,
3, 102; understanding left behind in
judging sublime 78–83
knowledge and knowing 14, 38, 57,
59

Lacan, Jacques 111
language and linguistics: Derrida's
analysis of Saussure's system 96;
God-talk 106; Lyotard on Kant
45–50; mediation of reality 28;
Milbank and 27–8, 34; and
ontology 37–50; technique 21;
utopian possibility 21
legislation: and moral law 14
Lessing, G.E. 16
Levinas, Emmanuel 108
liberals: pushed to choose between
nihilism and faith 27
liberation theology 5

Lindbeck, George 16
logic: of beauty and form 31–2; of
   exemplarity 68; of supplementarity
   68; of the unconscious 111
Long, Charles H. ix, 16–17
Luther, Martin 6, 15, 26–7
Lyotard, Jean-Francois: *The Differend*
   45–6, 48–9, 82, 99; effect of Kant
   2, 3, 64; failure of understanding
   78–9, 82; *Heidegger and "the jews"*
   50; imagination 78, 81–3, 92; Kant
   and *Critique of Judgment* 3, 44–50,
   85; *Lessons on the Analytic of the
   Sublime* 46, 47, 70–1, 75; logic of
   the unconscious 111; subjectivity 11,
   47–9, 69; sublime 46–50, 70–1, 102

MacIntyre, Alasdair 23–4, 29
Makkreel, Rudolf A. 73–4
Mallarmé, Stéphane 34
Marion, Jean-Luc 29–30, 34–5
mathematics 71–6, 81, 83, 89
Melville, Herman 34
Mendelssohn, Moses 2, 17
metaphysical tradition 20, 39, 97
Milbank, John: attack on Deleuze and
   Derrida 34; dissociation from
   philosophy 4; formlessness rejected
   29; and Kant 3, 23, 30; linguistics
   27–8, 34; and MacIntyre 23–4;
   Theology and Social Theory 24, 32;
   and transcendent 29, 35; and
   violence 24–7, 32–3
modernity: dissolution of sacred
   105–7; and postmodernity 10,
   108–9; shift from God to self 107;
   and violence 24–5
monogram 88–9
morality: anonymity feared by
   Milbank 28; beauty as symbol of
   89; and freedom 46; and
   imagination 75–6; intervention of
   reason 77; Kant 14, 30, 63, 103;
   MacIntyre 24; Tillich 13; *see also*
   ethics

nature: and evil 68; human
   understanding of 15; power of 72,
   76, 78; sublime 73
negative: imagination x, 73, 74, 83,
   91–2, 98; sublime 49; theology and
   God 106, 112
Neo-Platonism 25

Nietzsche, Friedrich: agonistic conflict
   32; *amor fati* 7; death of God 9;
   dissolution of modernity 10, 23,
   27
nihilism: grappling with 7, 23, 27–8,
   32
nuclear weapons 77

objectivity: causality 14–15; and
   judgment 4, 48, 69–70, 80;
   phenomenality 15, 56; relies on
   identity of subjectivity 56; schemata
   90; threatened by imagination 40;
   see also empirical realism
ontology 24, 32, 37–50, 93, 107, 111
orientation: and theology 16–21
Otto, Rudolph 19

Pascal, Blaise 72
Paton, H.J. 39–40, 86, 88
Paul: theology of 27
philosophy: ethics 23–4; formality and
   form 14–15; history of 14;
   marginalized in religious discourse
   6, 34; subjectivity and German
   philosophy 11; task of 22; *see also*
   transcendental philosophy
Pickstock, Catherine 23
piety: mistaken for faith 5–6
Plato 16, 24, 25
postmodern theology: of the body 111;
   French 6; and Kantian sublime 3,
   28, 29, 98; preoccupation with
   alterity 108–9; subjective turn of
   modernity deplored 108–9
postmodernism: inspiration of
   Nietzsche 23; method of asking
   questions of modernity 10; ontology
   of the body erotic 111
psychoanalysis xi, 5, 109–11

Radical Orthodoxy (Cambridge) ix–x,
   3, 23–36, 108
Raschke, Carl A. 111
reason and rationality: conflict with
   imagination 71–83; denial of
   sublime 29; destruction by Nietzsche
   23; Kant 17–18, 23, 43, 45–6, 48,
   63, 102; Lyotard 48; modern 24,
   33; modern loss of confidence in
   77; and morality 77; and orientation
   17
Reformation 25–6

Reimarus, H.S. 16
religion: appended to morality by Kant
    102–3; distinguished from
    superstition 72; identification a
    theological act 105; orientation to
    reality 17; popularity in USA 6;
    recognition of source of sublimity
    72–3; Tillich 4, 102–5
religious experience: existential
    character of 11–12; transcendental
    12–13
representation: failures of 31, 92;
    problem of sublime 83–4; *see also*
    transcendental imagination
Ricoeur, Paul 109
Rimbaud, Arthur 62
Roman Catholic Church: challenged
    by Luther 15, 26
Rousseau, Jean Jacques 67–8

sacred *see* Holy
Sallis, John 43, 77, 80, 102
Saussure, Ferdinand de 96
Schalow, Frank 41–3
Scharlemann, Robert P. 9, 106
Schelling, F.W.J. 87, 94–5
Schleiermacher, F.D.E. 19, 103, 108
secular: association with violence
    24–5; theology 20–1, 29–30, 35
self: consciousness of 38, 40, 42,
    54–8, 63–4; contested nature of
    9–11; crucial for theological
    discourse 100; death of 10–11; ego
    theory 9, 55, 62–3; empirical 13,
    55, 63; fractured 62–4; framework
    of 11; interiority of 62; negative
    imagination and 91; noumenal 55,
    63; replacement of God 100, 107;
    or subjectivity 5, 10, 100; and time
    60, 62–5, 92–3; transparency of
    9–11
Semler, J.S. 16
Shakespeare, William 34, 62
Sherover, Charles M. 38–9
Shoah see Holocaust
soul 55, 58
space 52–4, 57
spirituality: popularity of in USA 6
Strawson, P.F. 2, 55
subjectivity: beautiful judgments 83;
    dissolution of 107; German
    philosophy 11; God excluded
    29–30; Heidegger 11, 42, 50, 100;

human experience 53; I as empirical
    entity 55; Kant 5, 53, 55–8, 69;
    Lyotard 11, 47–9, 69; postmodern
    desire to abolish subject 108–9; self
    or 5, 10; and time 40, 54–5, 60,
    80–3
sublimation: failure of 109–10
sublime: disappearance of
    understanding in judgment of
    78–83; dynamical 71–3; failure of
    imagination 78, 80–1; formlessness
    of pure form 104–5; framed
    (Derrida) 77; intelligibility 112;
    judgment 4, 48–9, 75, 77, 80, 83–4;
    Kantian 3–5, 17–19, 22, 28–31,
    44–5, 50, 65, 67–84, 98, 103–4,
    109–12; Lyotard 46–50, 70–1, 102;
    mathematical 71–6, 81, 83, 89;
    Milbank's rejection 28; nature 72–3,
    76; negative pleasure 49; not
    correspondent to sublimation 109;
    theology of 4, 99–112;
    unrepresentable 19, 83–4; and the
    will 101
superstition 72
symbols 89–91
synthesis of recognition 79

Taylor, Charles 11
Taylor, Mark C. 9–10
theology: anthropology (Feuerbach)
    108; Barthianism 5; Church
    dogmatics 33; confessional 1, 33;
    conservative 6; content-driven or
    form-driven 3; crisis of 16; Death of
    God *see* Death of God theology;
    disorientation valued ix, 17–18, 33,
    104–5, 112; formal 16, 28;
    hermeneutical 91; Kantian critical
    philosophy as 9–22, 35; liberal 27;
    marginalization of philosophy and
    theory 6, 34, 35; negative 112;
    ontological structure 93, 107;
    philosophical 106; progressive or
    liberation (anti-intellectualism of) 5;
    Protestant 15; pure reason 91;
    radical 1–2, 19–20, 36; restricted to
    Christianity? 35–6; secular *see*
    secular theology; of sublime 4,
    99–112; threat to exceed bounds of
    revelation 1; Tillich and ultimate
    concern 1, 7, 11–13, 15, 35;
    transcendental *see* transcendental

theology; utopian 21; and Western imperialism 36; *see also* Radical Orthodoxy
Thirty Years War 26
Thomism *see* Aquinas
Tillich, Paul: *Biblical Religion and the Search for Ultimate Reality* 35; depth of reason 19; *Dynamics of Faith* 12; Kantianism of 13; knife edge between faith and doubt 27; morality 13; orientation 16–17; "Protestant principle" 6–7; religion as depth aspect of human spiritual life 4, 102–5; sign/symbol distinction 90; *Systematic Theology* 11, 12, 93; theological form 15; *Theology of Culture* 12, 103; ultimate concern ix, 1, 7, 11–13, 15, 16–17; understanding of self 5, 11–13
time: and absolute identity 93–4; Derrida 96–7; empirical appearances within 57; Heidegger 3, 38, 41–3, 53, 57, 60, 82, 92; imagination and 73–4; Kant 52–65, 89, 96–7; and self 60, 62–5, 92–3; and spirituality 40; and subjectivity 54–5, 80–3; transcendental determination of 54, 58, 92–4; and understanding 4, 94
Toulmin, Stephen 26
tradition: and theological thinking 19–20
transcendental argument 27–8, 38–44
transcendental idealism (Kant) 15, 94–5
transcendental imagination 4, 40, 43–4, 51–2, 57–62, 83–4, 85–98
transcendental philosophy 63, 78, 91
Transcendental Schematism 22, 40–1, 86
transcendental theology 12–13, 16, 22, 28, 29, 35

transcendental unity of apperception 42, 54–63, 79, 80, 92–3
Trinity: mythos that ensures order and harmony 33

ultimate concern ix, 1, 3, 7, 11–13, 15–17, 35, 102
understanding: categories 39, 48, 52, 88; left behind in judging sublime 4, 78–83; pure concepts of 55, 59; schematism 89–90; sensibility and 43; struggle with imagination 39, 64, 82, 86, 94; subjective process 38; temporality of 57
utopia: and new world order (globalization) 112; and secularity 20–1

Vahanian, Gabriel 20–1, 25
Vaihinger, Hans 2–3
Valla, Lorenzo 15
Vattimo, Gianni 10, 18–20
Verwindung 20
Vico, Giovanni Battista 34
violence: Christianity dissociated from 24–5; implication of modern thought in 24; Milbank's view of 24–7, 32–3; perpetuated by Christianity 25–7; symbol of cross 26–7
Von Balthasar *see* Balthasar, Hans Urs von

Whitehead, Alfred North 91, 94
will: Augustine's conception of 100–1
Winquist, Charles E. ix–xi, 12, 87, 91, 106
Wittgenstein, Ludwig 45
world wars: evil of 77

Young, J. Michael 87–8